Paragraph

A Journal of Modern Critical Theory

Volume 33, Number 2, July 2010

Rhythm in Literature after the Crisis in Verse

Edited by Peter Dayan and David Evans

Contents

Rhythm in Literature after the Crisis in Verse

PETER DAYAN AND DAVID EVANS

> There must be in the poem a number such that it prevents counting.
> Paul Claudel, *Cent phrases pour éventails* (*One hundred phrases for fans*).[1]

What is rhythm? Can there be a general theory of it? To the latter question, the obvious contemporary answer is no. There is nothing one can say about rhythm that engages with everything that we hold rhythm to be; depending on your point of view, it is either too broad a concept (perhaps, indeed, it is not a single concept at all), or too elusive. In the necessary absence of a general theory, theorising about rhythm, like attempts to define rhythm, can only be productive within a well-defined context. This volume, then, does not aim to say what rhythm is. But it does attempt to provide a theory, heretofore lacking, of how rhythm has functioned within precisely that literary tradition which one might see as responsible for our contemporary view of rhythm as impossible to theorise.

The slipperiness, the evasiveness, of the concept of rhythm in literature is, from the point of readers, poets, and critics, a relatively modern phenomenon. There seems to have been a time, one might say, in the literatures of all nations, when the producers and consumers of literature knew where to look, in the first place, for rhythm. Rhythm was something that happened in verse and thanks to the dynamics of verse; prosodic convention allowed us to appreciate it. Of course, no one would have denied that there was rhythm elsewhere, in prose as in music, but the rhythm of poetry was of a special kind, a higher kind than that in prose, and its connection with the rules of versification was unquestioned. That perceived privilege of the connection between rhythm and versification lasted until the nineteenth century. It was in France that its breakdown happened most clearly and most self-consciously. It was the French who most directly identified at the time what has, since 1885, been known as the 'crisis in verse'.

Paragraph 33:2 (2010) 147–157
DOI: 10.3366/E0264833410000817

Until then, French poetry, like poetry elsewhere, had been largely content with the age-old comfortable assumption that everyone knew what and where poetic rhythm was. When Baudelaire, for example, refers to rhythm and rhyme as the formal conditions of poetry, his definition of rhythm is inseparable from prosody.[2] However, that close-knit alliance of poetry, prosody, and rhythm can only hold for as long as poetry is taken to be essentially prosodic. As prose poetry, free verse, and more radical experiments with the spacing of words on the page began to assert their right to be considered poetic (Mallarmé's *Un Coup de dés* (*A Throw of the Dice*) was, after all, published with the subtitle 'Poème', and Baudelaire, having written poems in prose, hesitated between the titles *Le Spleen de Paris* (*Paris Spleen*) and *Petits poèmes en prose* (*Little Poems in Prose*)), they placed rhythm before a stark choice. When poetry divorces itself from the analysable conventions of prosody, rhythm must decide which of its two parents to follow. Will it remain rooted in prosody? in which case, non-prosodic poetry cannot be rhythmical; or will non-prosodic poetry proclaim itself as still rhythmical? in which case, prosody loses its claim to be the paradigmatic generator of rhythm.

A crisis in rhythm was, then, the immediate consequence of the crisis in verse which Mallarmé announced with memorable gravity in 'Crise de vers', a play on *crise de nerfs* (nervous breakdown). 'La littérature ici subit une exquise crise, fondamentale' (Literature is now undergoing an exquisite crisis, fundamental), he wrote.[3] As Mallarmé informed his audience in his Oxbridge lectures on 'La Musique et les Lettres': 'J'apporte en effet des nouvelles. Les plus surprenantes. Même cas ne se vit encore. — On a touché au vers' (Indeed, I bring most surprising news. The like of which has not been seen before. — Verse has been tampered with).[4] In this crisis, rhythm's choice was clear and decisive. It sided, not with traditional prosody, but with the new poetry, liberated from prosodic convention. Certainly, that is how post-crisis writers presented it. The concept of rhythm remained absolutely central to their attempts to describe the special quality of poetry and increasingly, as the distinction between poetry and other forms of literature became looser, of literature in general. As Apollinaire testified in 'Les Poètes d'aujourd'hui' (1909), 'le rythme a pris soudain une importance que les initiateurs, les destructeurs, les révolutionnaires si l'on veut de l'ancienne métrique n'avaient point soupçonnée' (suddenly, rhythm assumed an importance which the initiators, the destroyers, the revolutionaries if you will of the former metrics had not at all anticipated).[5] However, there seemed to be no means to analyse that rhythm as precisely as the study of versification had allowed the mechanics of prosody to be schematised. Nothing replaced prosody — except for a persistent analogy with music that remained as vague as the concept of rhythm itself, shifting from a conception of poetic rhythm as universal to one which could allow for an infinitely varied individuality. As Camille Mauclair claimed in Marinetti's *Enquête internationale sur le vers libre* (1909): 'Il y a autant de vers libres qu'il y a de poètes, et (. . .) leurs musiques ne se ressemblent pas' (There are as many kinds of free verse as there are poets, and (. . .) the music of each is unique).[6]

Mauclair, responding to an international 'enquête' or inquiry, did not distinguish between French poets, and poets of other nations. To him, as to the French in general, the crisis and its consequences, though born and first understood in France, were universal in their implications for poetry. In historical terms, there is, as we shall see, a sense in which this was never true: the link between prosody and poetry was not everywhere broken so easily, or in the same way. Nonetheless, one of the key features of the behaviour of rhythm in the French crisis was indeed replicated internationally: however poetry defined itself, whatever form it took, rhythm was perceived to remain an essential quality of it.

The theory that we aim to inaugurate in this volume, then, concerns the pervasiveness of rhythm after the crisis of verse; the reasons for which rhythm remained such a persistent reference point in literature despite the loss of its prosodic moorings. It seemed to us that, whereas the critical literature overflows with many excellent, precise and detailed analyses of the rhythms of specific poetic and literary texts, no serious attempt to arrive at a theoretical discourse explaining the enduring importance of rhythm as a concept had yet been attempted. One obstacle to the construction of such a discourse could be described as a sort of hangover from the days of prosody. Contemporary critical work on the concept of rhythm in poetry remains profoundly rooted in the analysis of national traditions. In France, for example, over the last twenty years, the most striking and influential evolution in the critical understanding of poetic rhythm has resulted from the creation of a new technique for analysing metre in French verse, 'métrico-métrie', by Benoît de Cornulier and the Centre d'Études Métriques at the Université de Nantes.[7] Where theories of rhythm have sought to emancipate themselves from this prosodic focus, they have unfortunately not been able to replace it with any other focus in literature. Covering a much wider variety of rhythmic contexts than Cornulier, Henri Meschonnic's formidable *Critique du rythme* remains a defining work in the field over twenty-five years after its first publication. Boldly rejecting any correspondences between rhythms in literature and those of the body or the natural world, Meschonnic analyses rhythm in a wide variety of sources including newspaper articles as well as literary texts. Unlike Cornulier, he locates rhythm in language in all its forms. But like Cornulier, he fails to explain just what makes a literary rhythm, as opposed to any other kind;[8] his work, though magnificent as a critique, gives no foothold for a theory of rhythm in literature.

Seen from the point of view of post-crisis literature, this seems to us an inevitable limitation of any critical approach that focuses solely on rhythm in language, especially within a single language. The truly distinctive impulse of post-crisis poets is their determination to suggest the existence of a kind of rhythm whose relationship with the actual tangible dynamics of language is resolutely and cunningly elusive, a rhythm which somehow escapes every one of the wide variety of analytical frameworks which scholars might attempt to impose on it. It figures itself never as simply within poetry, but always as between discourses, media, or types of experience. For that reason, it refuses to settle within the purview of any disciplinary approach. Indeed, it evades the scientific as well as the linguistic — not to mention the musicological. To give a particularly interesting recent example: in January 2009, a special issue of the scientific journal *Cortex* appeared, entitled *The Rhythmic Brain*. Its introduction begins thus: 'Music is a universal but still poorly understood form of human communication in which abstract patterns of sound can cause people to cry, laugh, dance, reflect, bond and even mate. Rhythm is a basic organising principle of music.'[9] This seems reasonable, as does the implication that rhythm can be analysed as an organising principle within the medium of music. The rest of the issue continues to assume a certain working definition of 'music' as containing, precisely, 'patterns', within which rhythm can be analysed as an 'organising principle'. This analysable patterning, however, corresponds to the very definition of rhythm that the crisis in verse aimed to contest. It would perhaps not be illegitimate to perceive the extraordinary success of that contestation in the difficulty which the *Cortex* team found in trying to reach a consensus on where rhythm is actually to be located:

The editorial process was extremely interesting and even challenging, not least since the word rhythm can mean different things to different people, while terms such as beat, metrical/non-metrical, simple/complex rhythm, conventional/ unconventional rhythm and so forth, can be the topic of heated debate.[10]

The question is: can this challenge be met by further research into the nature of rhythm within any given medium? Or does rhythm, as we conceive it post-crisis, actually contain a constitutive resistance to all such research? We have assumed the latter: it seems that the more rigorous, the more scientific one attempts to be, the less able one is to cope with the meaning of rhythm in post-crisis verse. The solution to the problem, we thought, would be to approach it, not from one point of view, but from several simultaneously.

Our idea, then, was, for the first time, perhaps, to bring together studies on literature in different European languages around the concept of rhythm in the post-crisis period, referring (always, centrally) to poetry, but also to many different media and kinds of experience described as rhythmic. We trusted that this multi-cultural approach would provide a healthy remedy to the inward-looking tendency of the ways in which rhythm has hitherto been conceptualised and theorised, and would suit the topic particularly well in that, precisely, what rhythm seems to do after the crisis in verse is to slip its anchor in analysable specifics — in the first place the specifics of a given language, but also, more subtly, in verbal language in general. We also hoped that the differences between the history of the crisis in different national traditions would prevent us from settling into comfortable assumptions about rhythm's relocation after the divorce between poetry and metrical convention. And so it proved.

The project was thus from the outset conceived of as an interchange around a central question, in which a diversity of perspectives would not only keep consensus productively at bay, but would continually lead back to the reasons for rhythm's elusiveness. We therefore began the project with live debate: two memorable study days in Edinburgh, during which first drafts of all the papers in this volume were presented, chewed over, and discussed with a steadily increasing sense of the richness and complexity of the subject, and its refusal of all stable conceptualisation.[11] Arriving at conclusions was not the order of the day. But the discussion certainly did fulfil our aim of bringing out the way that rhythm becomes both central to literature and endlessly slippery as a concept after the crisis in verse; and the variety of national traditions equally certainly served to question single-language-centred assumptions.

David Gascoigne's presentation of the multi-lingual and sometimes, one might say, anti-lingual movement that was Dada demonstrated how rhythm was kept alive by artists of radically contrasting aesthetic persuasions, by situating it somewhere before, above, or beyond language conceived of as a means of making sense. It could, rejecting words entirely, be in drum-beats (would that be poetry? would the question matter?); it could also be found in poems largely written in words unknown to linguists, whose similarity to what the Dadaists called 'negro' (i.e. primitive) poetry was intended to suggest the existence of fundamental human rhythms, obscured by Western civilisation, whose specific qualities, of course, the Dadaist was careful never to elucidate. David Gascoigne showed that it is always possible to find a way to explain how we create rhythm from such texts, how we find strong and weak beats, for example, and this, in poetry, always depends on our understanding of language and its morphology. As soon as there is anything that looks like language, in other words, rhythm depends on our understanding of it. Yet Dada decisively breaks any link between that understanding and the sense of a national tradition that validates it. Rhythm is essential to Dada; but equally essential is the refusal of any stable context that would allow any evaluation of that rhythm, any appreciation of what it is or why it works as literary. A Dada rhythm might as well be African as French, German, or English; so it is really, plainly, none of those, and it can be situated precisely nowhere. That is how rhythm contributes to the great Dada enterprise: we are convinced it is there, but we become ridiculous as soon as we try to say what or where it is.

Dada's multi-lingual iconoclasm contrasted strikingly with the history of Russian verse, presented by Barry Scherr. The prosodic conventions of nineteenth-century Russian art poetry did not have the ancient roots in the language that French, German, British or Italians claimed for their verse; but, after a period of experimentation around the time of the Revolution, they survived far more generally into the twentieth century, thanks to the cultural conservatism both of the Bolsheviks and of their emigré opponents. However, in that context, when poets of the middle of the twentieth century were brave enough to disrupt conventional rhythm, the effect was to bring the issues around rhythm into the starkest possible relief. Prosody, for them, could not be disentangled from its socio-political implications; any refusal of it immediately brought to the fore the question of what poetry might be apart from its social function, and the indeterminate nature of non-prosodic rhythm becomes, not merely observable, but an always disturbing presence.

This sense of disturbance was less often immediately evident in French and English literature thanks, it seemed, to a tactic that strangely emerged as, in a way, common to Virginia Woolf (as presented by Emma Sutton) and Paul Valéry (David Evans's subject). Both imply that rhythm, for the writer, somehow precedes words. Valéry describes himself feeling a rhythm, discovering a rhythm, before the words of the poem appear to materialise it; Woolf makes of the precedence of rhythm a principle of literature, describing words being put 'on the backs of rhythm'. This might be taken to suggest, contrary to our initial assumption, that post-crisis poetic rhythm is not, in fact, elusive and indeterminate; that it can have a solid presence of its own, which the poet perceives and materialises. This would be comfortingly similar to the old idea of prosodic rhythm, whereby the linguistic rhythms as manifested in the text fulfil formal conditions which precede composition. However, careful analysis of the context of these described experiences of rhythm-preceding-words shows how problematic they remain. No rhythm exists without a material in which to manifest itself; that much is clear, as is the self-conscious craftsmanship to which both authors devoted a great deal of time and effort. The much admired artful work with the matter of words, by Valéry and by Woolf, is clear evidence of this; indeed, Valéry is perfectly conscious of it, and describes the process of poetic composition from the outset as one of working with and through the peculiar properties of the French language in all its rich detailing. On a larger scale, in *The Voyage Out*, the presence, absence, and functioning of rhythm depend, in fact, on many oppositions that are plainly verbally mediated, not the least of which is a complex gender politics. The material of the rhythm before words remains intangible; whereas the rhythm that Woolf and Valéry create actually depends on the material characteristics of the words in which they create it. One cannot, therefore, conceptualise it as a pre-existent rhythm which the words subsequently clothe, so to speak. Once one has followed the logic of their presentation of rhythm through to this point, the disturbing force of rhythm re-emerges. As forcefully as in the Russian poets' work, rhythm comes to represent something that is as elusive in its source and matter as it is essential to literature; it not only invites disruption, it actually is disruption, disruption of our common sense of how we ought to be able to understand and situate the value of what we read.

Simon Jarvis, after reading out John Wilkinson's *The Speaking Twins* (an unforgettable moment), contributed another way of interpreting the experience of Valéry or Woolf. Wilkinson's verse rhythms fiercely resist conceptualisation, and yet remain irresistible, unmistakable, vigorous, determined. This ceases to appear critically problematic if one accepts that just as, for more than a century, musicians have maintained that they can think, non-verbally, in music — 'penser musicalement', according to Debussy's expression[12] — so we might accept that there is 'thinking in rhythm'. This seems, indeed, to be the experience of many poets, and of many readers; and close analysis of the way we respond to poetry confirms this. Post-crisis, however, 'thinking in rhythm' cannot be neatly aligned with any definable kind of rhythm; and the problem remains of determining which rhythms, if any, are specifically those of poetry, or perhaps even more problematically, of literature.

On that subject, the example of Dino Campana, analysed by Helen Abbott, was eloquent. It is plain that for him, rhythm in itself is not necessarily good or bad, poetic or unpoetic. Rhythm can be perceived as something repetitive, tired, and mundane; or, on the contrary, musical, magic, sacred. It can shade into a weary trudge, or into the walk of a beautiful woman. These opposing rhythmical modes reveal obsessions which shape poetic rhythm, but do not define it. The distinguishing characteristic of the poetic rhythm seems to be nothing more precise than a certain power to invite the imagination onwards, towards a point beyond the present, where easily perceptible rhythm is absorbed into something that transcends it, as the rhythm of water can become a flow.

Rhythm thus becomes dependent, not merely on specific properties present in the material, but also on a movement of the imagination that actually leads to a dissolving of those properties. Similarly, the key to the reading of Julio Cortázar's *Los Premios* offered by Carolina Orloff and Peter Dayan became an imaginary rhythm which, in the end, denies its own roots in the material. Pre-crisis rhythm can be analysed as an objective property of verse or music; but rhythm in *Los Premios* turns out not to be an objective property of anything. Generally speaking, the novel's protagonists are thoroughly sceptical of the possibility that rhythm might have any real presence in their lives. The only character who is convinced that rhythm, the rhythm of poetry or of music, is also an objective property of the world, is presented as out on a limb and intellectually unconvincing. Yet there are certain kinds of experience that seem able to change people's minds, temporarily at least: falling in love; and art — including, perhaps, reading *Los Premios*. Both require a conviction, not unlike that of Valéry, Woolf, or Campana, that there exists a rhythm, a rhythm before any specific words, which makes a certain kind of sense of the world — a sense qualitatively different from the kind of meaning that words might make without it. However, that conviction, in *Los Premios*, remains unstable. People fall out of love as easily as they fall in love; rhythm vanishes as quickly as it appears, and as it vanishes, we see that the sceptical characters, though they were wrong to deny the importance of rhythm, were right not to believe in its fixed presence in the real world. That instability mirrors both the ambiguity of rhythm in Campana's verse, and the difficulty of conceptualising the rhythm in literature that might have existed before the words that materialise it. Rhythm remains something central to art, and yet curiously, perhaps infuriatingly, and certainly healthily, resistant to becoming a discernable object of any truth-discourse.

Eric Prieto's subtle analysis of Jacques Réda's versification showed how even within verse that continues to depend on (though not simply to reproduce) the good old conventions of prosody, post-crisis rhythm can retain that paradoxical character: it remains indubitably central, and indubitably linked, somehow, to analysable features of the work, and yet at the same time it is endlessly slippery whenever we try to pin down its presence as a verifiable truth. Réda's contribution to the maintenance of that paradoxical character expresses itself in his interweaving of the individual, the personal, with the traditional. His verse is based on his own modern re-shaping of traditional prosodic functions; particularly, the standard syllable count which was the staple of French metrics for centuries before the crisis. However, through an analogy with jazz rhythms and the semi-improvisatory aspect of swing, Réda introduces a perspective which links rhythm in poetry to a phenomenological and post-structuralist discourse on rhythm emphasising its necessary rôle in the construction of the subject; this in turn poses the question of the individual in art. We are nothing without rhythm; but is the rhythm we need uniquely ours? Réda's rhythm certainly has characteristics which are, recognisably and demonstrably, uniquely his. Furthermore, his verse, like jazz, is also happy to allow a certain personal rhythmic freedom to the interpreter. And yet, as Eric Prieto pointed out, just as important to Réda as the individuality of rhythm are the limits to that individuality. The jazz with which he identifies is not simply improvisation, not the 'free jazz' of, say, Ornette Coleman. Similarly, the rhythms of his poetry are not entirely free; he is not entirely free to choose them. Simon Jarvis describes Wilkinson's work as 'unfree verse', and not only because poetic rhythm requires constraints; it is also because rhythm in literature, after the crisis in verse, always comes from elsewhere, comes upon the poem from elsewhere. It is indeed, as Valéry implied, felt to precede words, perhaps to emerge from the world outside or beyond the poet, perhaps to speak for the primitive or even the universal; its manifestations are stubbornly individual, but it is never entirely under the control of the individual.

Any theory of such a rhythm must have the courage in the first place to confront, without resolving them, the innumerable paradoxes that have given it its distinctive place in literary discourse. Rather than trying to understand what rhythm is — an obviously impossible task — we should ask ourselves instead why literature seems to feed endlessly on a kind of thinking that is summed up under that word 'rhythm'; and what, if any, are the constant, or at least typical, dynamics of its operation. Our aim in these essays is, then, to seek, not for the truth of rhythm, but for the way it has served the purposes of all those writers who, like us, cannot escape the conviction that 'it don't mean a thing if it ain't got that swing'. It is to rhythm itself that we would like to dedicate this volume.

NOTES

1   Paris, Gallimard, coll. 'Poésie', 1996, n. p.
2   See the essays 'Théophile Gautier' and 'Auguste Barbier', in Charles Baudelaire, *Œuvres complètes*, 2 vols, edited by Claude Pichois (Paris: Gallimard, coll. 'Bibliothèque de la Pléiade', 1975–76), II, 105 and 145.
3   Stéphane Mallarmé, *Œuvres complètes*, 2 vols, edited by Bertrand Marchal (Paris: Gallimard, coll. 'Bibliothèque de la Pléiade', 1998–2003), II, 205.
4   Ibid., II, 64.
5   Guillaume Apollinaire, *Œuvres en prose complètes*, edited by Pierre Caizergues and Michel Décaudin, 3 vols (Paris: Gallimard, coll. 'Bibliothèque de la Pléiade', 1977–93), II, 915.
6   Milan, Editions de Poesia, 1909.
7   For a selection of excellent studies on French metrics, see Jean Mazaleyrat, *Pour une étude rythmique du vers français moderne* (Paris: Lettres Modernes Minard, 1963) and *Éléments de métrique française* (Paris: Armand Colin, 1974); Jacques Roubaud, 'Mètre et vers (Deux applications de la métrique générative de Halle-Keyser)', *Poétique* 7 (1971), 366–87 and *La Vieillesse d'Alexandre, essai sur quelques états récents du vers français* (Paris: Maspéro, 1978); Benoît de Cornulier, *Théorie du vers: Rimbaud, Verlaine, Mallarmé* (Paris: Éditions du Seuil, 1982) and *Art poétique: notions et problèmes de métrique* (Lyon: Presses Universitaires de Lyon, 1995); *Le Vers français: Histoire, théorie, esthétique*, edited by Michel Murat (Paris: Champion, 1999), as part of Champion's series 'Métrique française et comparée'; Jean-Michel Gouvard, *La Versification* (Paris: Presses Universitaires de France, 1999) and *Critique du*

vers (Paris: Champion, 2000); Marc Dominicy, *Le Souci des apparences: huit études de poétique et de métrique* (Brussels: Éditions de l'Université, 1989); Valérie Beaudouin, *Mètre et rythmes du vers classique. Corneille et Racine* (Paris: Champion, 2002); *Métrique française et métrique accentuelle*, edited by Dominique Billy, Benoît de Cornulier and Jean-Michel Gouvard, special issue of *Langue française* 99 (1993); Clive Scott, *A Question of Syllables* (Cambridge: Cambridge University Press, 1986) and *Reading the Rhythm: The Poetics of French Free Verse 1910–1930* (Oxford: Clarendon Press, 1993).

8   See Henri Meschonnic, *Critique du rythme: anthropologie historique du langage* (Lagrasse: Verdier, 1982), *Le Rythme et la vie* (Lagrasse: Verdier, 1989) and *Politique du rythme, politique du sujet* (Lagrasse: Verdier, 1995); Henri Meschonnic and Gérard Dessons, *Traité du rythme: du vers et des proses*, (Paris: Armand Colin, 2005 [1998]). For approaches to rhythm which locate a text's rhythmicity in variables drawn from linguistics, see Nicolas Ruwet, Jean-Michel Gouvard and Marc Dominicy, *Linguistique et poétique*, special edition of *Langue française* 110 (1996); Christine Michaux and Marc Dominicy, *Linguistic Approaches to Poetry*, special edition of *Belgian Journal of Linguistics* 15 (2001); *Rythmes*, edited by Lucie Bourassa, special edition of *Protée* 18 : 1 (1990); Lucie Bourassa, *Rythme et sens: Des processus rythmiques en poésie contemporaine* (Montreal: Les Éditions Balzac, 1993); Éliane Delente, *Le Rythme: Principe d'organisation du discours poétique*, doctoral thesis (Université de Caen, Linguistique française, 1992); Roger Pensom, *Accent and Metre in French: a history of the relation between linguistic accent and metrical practice in French, 1100–1900* (Bern: Peter Lang, 1998). Paul Fraisse, in *Psychologie du rythme* (Paris: Presses Universitaires de France, 1974) proposes a psychological explanation for the importance of rhythm, while other studies such as Frédéric Deloffre, *Le Rythme de la prose: objet et méthodes de l'analyse* (The Hague: 1966; no publisher given) and *Rhythms: Essays in French Literature, Thought and Culture*, edited by Elizabeth Lindley and Laura MacMahon (Bern: Peter Lang, 2008) see rhythm at work across a wide variety of texts, far beyond the metrical.

9   Katie Overy and Robert Turner, 'Introduction', *Cortex* 45 (2009), 1.

10   Ibid.

11   We are extremely grateful to the British Academy for its generous funding of these study days.

12   In more than one letter of 1915; see, for example, his *Correspondance 1884–1918*, edited by F. Lesure (Paris: Hermann, 1993), 358.

Paul Valéry and the Search for Poetic Rhythm

DAVID EVANS

Abstract:
Throughout his theoretical writings, Valéry insists on two fundamental principles: poetic rhythm is undefinable and yet it is central to poetry. Although his verse practice evolves from irregularity to regularity, Valéry insists that predictable metrical forms are no guarantee of poeticity, and rejects the Romantic model of rhythmic mimesis based on the cosmos, nature or the human body. It is not by confirming the meaningfulness of regular patterns, therefore, that poetic rhythm signifies; rather, the complex overlapping of multiple, elusive and unanalysable rhythms provides a source of questions to which the answer is constantly deferred; and that, for Valéry, is the definition of poetry.

Keywords: Valéry, *Cahiers*, rhythm, rhyme, versification, metre, beauty, constellations, deferral

The work of Paul Valéry (1871–1945) emerges from and contributes to a radical reconceptualisation of poetic rhythm, beginning with his acquaintance with Mallarmé, and a passion for his poetry, in the 1890s. Although Valéry's poetic production was quite limited, his theoretical writings filled countless notebooks (*cahiers*) with detailed reflections on the processes of composition and reading; while his verse amounts to the short monologue *La Jeune Parque* (*The Young Fate*), a brief *Album de vers anciens* (*Album of Old Verses*) and the twenty-one poems of *Charmes* (*Charms*), he wrote the *Cahiers* without interruption from the late 1890s to his death. Valéry offers some of the most rigorous, lucid, complex and above all, healthily sceptical thinking on the meaning of post-crisis rhythm. His analysis is not limited to literature — he explores rhythm as a characteristic of memory, motor functions, perception, the natural world, as well as in the composition and reception of the arts — but given the vast scope, and sheer amount, of Valéry's writings on the subject, I will restrict myself here to his analyses of rhythm as a central feature of poetry. Valéry's thinking is invaluable because, first and foremost, he insists throughout his life on

Paragraph 33:2 (2010) 158–175
DOI: 10.3366/E0264833410000829

the impossibility of defining rhythm satisfactorily:

> *Rhythm.* Very hard to analyse, this notion. (*Cahiers*, 1914–15, V, 499)[1]
>
> This word 'rhythm' is not clear to me. (*Cahiers*, 1915, V, 541)
>
> I have read or composed twenty 'definitions' of *Rhythm*, none of which I adopt. (Œ, I, 1289)
>
> Rhythm — no objective definition. To define it would be to produce it. (*Cahiers*, 1938, XXI, 14)

While acknowledging rhythm's undefinability, though, Valéry never ceases investigating it as a scholar and poet, constantly questioning the value of metrical verse. The eighteen-year old Valéry writes to Charles Boès in 1889, 'I believe in the all-powerfulness of rhythm' (Œ, I, 1574) and line five of 'Orphée' (1891 version) reads: 'Le dieu chante, et selon le rythme tout puissant' (the god sings, and by the all-powerful rhythm); and while this youthful enthusiasm for rhythm never abates, the relationship between rhythm, poetry and verse is never taken for granted.

The *Album de vers anciens* (1920) contains poems mostly written between 1890 and 1893 in traditional metrical form: mainly alexandrines, the centuries-old twelve-syllable line with an obligatory pause, or caesura, halfway through coinciding with a break in the sense: 'Le chant clair des rameurs / enchaîne le tumulte' (The clear song of the rowers enslaves the tumult) ('Hélène', l. 11). Yet within that regular form, in keeping with a precedent set, notably, by Baudelaire, Rimbaud, Verlaine, Banville, Laforgue and Mallarmé, Valéry includes an extremely high proportion of ametrical lines, where the caesura falls mid-word or after an unaccentuable schwa.[2] Moreover, many of these metrically irregular lines deal with music and nature, suggesting that poetic rhythm does not lie in an outdated Romantic analogy between a musical universe and metrical verse:

> Où le jardin mé**lo** / dieux se dodeline ('La Fileuse', l.3)
> (Where the melodious garden nods its head)
>
> Les hauts murs d'or har**mo** / nieux d'un sanctuaire ('Orphée', l.9)
> (The high walls, of harmonious gold, of a sanctuary)
>
> Une goutte tomb**e** / de la flûte sur l'eau ('Épisode', l.18)
> (A drop falls from the flute onto the water)
>
> Entendre l'onde **se** / rompre aux degrés sonores ('Hélène', l.2)
> (Hearing the wave break in sonorous degrees)

In this last example, the rhythms of metrical verse and the waves are in conflict, breaking the anticipated balance of the line rather than mapping onto each other as in Victor Hugo, for example. Similar rhythmic disturbances occur at the line end, with *enjambement* displacing the accent from the rhyme word to the next line: 'que l'Océan constelle / D'écume' ('which the Ocean constellates / With spray', 'Été', ll.29–30). Whereas the rhythms of the sea are synonymous with verse in Romantic poetry, here the sea-spray, scattered in the air, disturbs rather than confirms metrical structures. Poetic rhythm, for Valéry, may be all-powerful, but already in his early verse, it is clearly not synonymous with predictable, fixed metre and rhyme.

While the early twentieth century saw French free verse blossom, Valéry's verse seemed to return to regularity. *La Jeune Parque* (1917), on which Valéry worked while editing his early verse, is remarkable for alexandrines where syntax and metre coincide, and from over 500 lines, almost all observe a strong caesura and a firm 6–6 rhythm. As Valéry explained in 1941, 'I insisted (...) on observing the rules of classical prosody, on being even more rigorous, perhaps' (*Œ*, I, 1614). Similarly, *Charmes* (1922), which Valéry describes as 'a collection of prosodic experiments',[3] displays a wide variety of canonical stanzaic and metrical forms from pentasyllable to dodecasyllable, all with their roots in the French tradition stretching back to the late medieval period and the Renaissance, and with several influenced by Hugo. As well as their hearty embrace of metrical structures, the last two volumes are noteworthy for the frequency of *rimes léonines*, extremely rich rhymes whose rhyming phonemes stretch over two or more syllables, strengthening the parallelism between isometric lines, an effect further emphasised by the short metres:

> Fin suprême, étin**cellement** (...)
> Proclame univer**sellement** ('Ode secrète', ll.21–4)

It would be tempting to interpret this enthusiasm for reinforcing metrical structures as a return to a simplistic belief in rhythmic regularity and traditional verse form. Valéry insists, however, that the poetic value of regularity is unstable, arguing in his *cahiers* that 'The principle is the music of verse. Rhyme richness can contribute to it. It can also detract from it' (*Cahiers*, 1914, V, 273). Furthermore, in his writings on poetry he constantly classifies rhythm separately from metre and number when discussing formal techniques, such as 'rhythmics, metrics and prosody' ('Questions de poésie', *Œ*, I, 1293).

Indeed, Valéry clearly states that 'Feeling the rhythm or the non-rhythm is entirely independent from the counting (dénombrement)' (*Cahiers*, 1915, V,543).

Intriguingly, given the evolution of his verse practice towards predictable regularity, Valéry repeatedly equates the mechanisms of metrical verse with the death of poetry. Bad verse, he writes, gives the impression of being an 'automatic mechanism' (*Cahiers*, 1910, IV: 485), and of Hugo's verse he writes disparagingly, 'nothing is more strictly mechanical' (*Cahiers*, 1915, V, 667). When Boileau codified verse, this was seized upon by inferior minds, who 'could prove by counting on their fingers that the verse was good' (*Cahiers*, 1917, VI, 748). Thus, he argues:

The classical rules of French verse — almost impossible to justify as a whole, easy to remember like a decree, difficult to observe without writing nonsense, since most of one's art is spent on satisfying them; their clarity allowing someone, with no ear and with no poetry, to judge poets; conventional rules; societal; very likely to make for ridiculous verse, to submit the man who sings to the man who can count to twelve. (*Cahiers*, 1916, VI, 202)

Similarly, despite his own extravagantly rich rhymes in *Charmes*, Valéry disagrees with 'the idea of making rich rhyme a mechanical criterion. An artist whoever respected it. Not an artist whoever sacrificed it' (*Cahiers*, 1914, V, 273). The mistake of the Parnassian school, for Valéry, lay in their defining too rigidly the formal elements of beauty:

They defined the 'beautiful line of verse' too precisely. As a result, any poet could measure himself accurately by the overall amount of his verse compared to the number of beautiful lines. (...) Whenever beauty becomes determined like that, it becomes facile. (*Cahiers*, 1915, V, 882)

For Valéry, it is this excessive formal prescriptivism which precipitated the crisis in French verse, whereas what is needed now, on the contrary, is 'la beauté informulée' (unformulated beauty) which depends on 'ce qui reste d'informe' (what remains of the formless). In his important 'Discours sur l'esthétique' (1937), Valéry observes that Beauty will always elude scientific analysis, since no formula can account for, or prescribe, a sufficiently wide variety: 'The very idea of a "Science of Beauty" was destined to be undermined by the diversity of beauties produced or recognised in the world over time' (Œ, I, 1302).

While Valéry does not in practice discard regular metrical conventions, then, these conventions do not provide the rhythmic proof of poetry, nor does their presence in a work guarantee its poeticity. Rather, just as Virginia Woolf, in the epigraph to Emma Sutton's essay in this volume, presents rhythm as a wave, not monotonously regular, but rather, breaking and tumbling in the mind, Valéry argues that poetry be redefined as an 'undulatory mechanism!' (*Cahiers*, 1927, XII, 275). The notion of a mechanical device remains, but in practice, poetic rhythm requires the performance of a regularity which the skill of the poet must somehow make us forget: 'How ridiculous the scansion of metrical verse — Reducing music to beating time, whereas music consists of making you forget the beat while nonetheless sticking to it rigorously' (*Cahiers*, 1940, XXIII, 197). The active, multiple nature of this new rhythmical model is highlighted by Valéry's explanation of how rhythm functions in a succession of rhymed alexandrine couplets such as those of *La Jeune Parque*, which adheres to the conventional alternation of masculine (ending in a consonant) and feminine (ending in an 'e') rhymes:

There is a sort of rhythm particular to the alexandrine which lies in the combination of the phrase and the rhyme — you have in the series MMFFMMFFMMFF the combinations MM, or FF, or MF, or FM, ie. a perfect couplet MM, FF, or a mixed couplet FM, MF.

This rhythm is in addition to all the other kinds of rhythms. (*Cahiers*, 1918, VII, 636)

Conventional verse, then, provides a framework in which multiple rhythms are superimposed and performed simultaneously, set to work with and against each other as an irresolvable process, and it is this complexity which defines the experience of poetic rhythm for Valéry; free verse lacks the basic metrical blueprint against which other patterns can be experienced in counterpoint.[4]

The fallacy of rhythmic mimesis

One of the most crucial features of Valéry's thinking on rhythm, in terms of his importance to the post-Mallarmean poetic landscape, is his refusal to see any meaning in the natural world beyond that which the human mind attributes to it, thereby severing any Romantic links between verse form and the cosmos.[5] For Hugo, the stars explicitly proclaim God's presence in the universe:

> — Pléiades qui percez nos voiles,
> Qu'est-ce que disent vos étoiles?
> — Dieu! dit la constellation. ('Les Mages', ll. 18–20)[6]

('Pleiades, which pierce our veils,
What do your stars express?'
'God!' replies the constellation.)

By contrast, in a famous passage from Valéry's writings on Mallarmé, he recalls walking with the author of the recently completed experimental poem *Un Coup de dés* (*A Throw of the Dice*), and contemplating the stars, which seem to be 'the very text of the silent universe; a text full of clarity and enigmas; as tragic, as indifferent as you like; which speaks and does not speak; a tissue of multiple meanings; which assembles order and disorder; which proclaims a God as powerfully as it denies Him' ('*Un Coup de dés*', 1920, Œ, I, 626). The constellations are neither a random, meaningless jumble, nor proof of a divine presence; it is their very inscrutability which is so captivating, tempting us to see meaningful structures where there may be none at all. Yet since the absence of meaning, in the great French tradition of Pascal and Baudelaire, is a terrifying prospect, it is only human to impose order on the cosmos, as Valéry confirms in 'Ode secrète', from *Charmes*:

> O quel Taureau, quel Chien, quelle Ourse,
> Quels objets de victoire énorme,
> Quand elle entre aux temps sans ressource
> L'âme impose à l'espace informe! (ll.17–20)
> (Oh what a Bull, what a Dog, what a Bear,
> What objects of great victory,
> When it enters times of no resource,
> The soul imposes on formless space!)

Un Coup de dés itself appeared to Valéry 'comme si une constellation eût paru qui eût enfin signifié quelque chose' (Œ, I, 624) (as if a constellation had appeared which at last meant something), the pair of imperfect subjunctives maintaining the necessary ambiguity whereby meaning, in the world as in the text, is no longer a stable truth, but rather a tantalizing yet never fully realised possibility. If poetic rhythm, therefore, shares anything with the stars, it is that they both give us the suspicion that meaning is in there somewhere; they inspire us to search for it, tempt us to impose patterns and structures on them, and yet never confirm whether those patterns have any intrinsic value. A defining characteristic of post-crisis rhythm is, similarly, its fundamental resistance to the decoding which it actively invites us to attempt.

As well as the stars, another timeless image traditionally presented as embodying the rhythms of the natural world is the sea, with its tidal motion, wave patterns, storms and calm passages making it a tempting metaphor for verse. Walter Ince, for example, claims that 'in the concluding lines of *La Jeune Parque*, the rhythms do not just "suggest" the disordered power of wave and water, they are it, transposed into a linguistic experience', while Christine Crow hears 'the ebb-and-flow rhythm of the sea in the alexandrine'.[7] Yet for Valéry, the sea could represent 'an oscillation limited in itself', 'a regular phase'; 'The drama, strange at first, seems in its repetition like a machine' (*Cahiers*, 1911, IV, 503). Valéry rejects the idea that marine rhythms contain any meaning beyond themselves, arguing that regular rhythms are not necessarily inherent in the waves, but rather, are imposed on their complex structures by a human sensibility in search of reassuring order: 'It is impossible, in my opinion, to *reduce rhythm to objective observation*. That is why I dislike the term *Rhythm of the waves* which eliminates the *senses*' (*Cahiers*, 1935, XVIII, 83). Thus, in the final stanza of 'Le Cimetière marin', after twenty-three stanzas of intense intellectual activity, scrutiny of the natural world, and contemplation of mortality, the wind picks up, disturbing the poet's book, and the joyful waves break the calm waters, shattering the poet's reverie; at this very moment, the traditional 4/6 rhythm of the decasyllable, which has been scrupulously respected in the previous 142 lines, is disrupted by a *césure lyrique* which places an unaccentuable word-final schwa at the accented fourth syllable. Moreover, recalling the recurrent presence of the sea in the aforementioned metrical disturbances of the *Album de vers anciens*, it is the unaccentuable 'e' of 'vagues' (waves) itself, after an imperative — 'Rompez' (Break) — which explicitly calls for structural dismantling:

> L'air immense ouvre / et referme mon livre,
> La vague en poudre / ose jaillir des rocs!
> Envolez-vous, / pages tout éblouies!
> Rompez, vag**ues**! / Rompez d'eaux réjouies (ll.140–43)
> (The immense air opens and shuts my book,
> The powdery wave dares to spring from the rocks!
> Fly away, dazzled pages!
> Break, waves! Break with joyful waters)

In striking contrast with the Romantic belief in the quasi-versificatory rhythms of the natural world — for Hugo, 'nature is a symphony; there is rhythm and measure everywhere; and you could almost believe that God had made the world in verse'[8]—here Valéry suggests a fundamental incompatibility between the sea's unpredictable structures and the fixed metrical forms of verse, which was already highlighted by Rimbaud in 'Le Bateau ivre' ('The Drunken Boat'), where the unruly waters engulf and erase the poem's metrical structure. When Valéry's Parque contemplates the waves, searching for the truth of her human condition, she finds that 'la houle me murmure une ombre de reproche' (the swell murmurs a hint of a reproach at me);[9] and in 'Un feu distinct...', from the *Album de vers anciens,* instead of confirming the meaningfulness of regular rhythm, the sound of the waves inspires only doubt:

> Comme à la vide conque un murmure de mer,
> Le doute (ll.12–13)
> (As to the empty shell a murmur of the sea
> Doubt)

Thirdly, it often proves extremely tempting for poets and critics alike to imagine a rhythmic truth in the human body, in what appear to be the regular rhythms of our breathing, heartbeat and pulse. Yet while Valéry reflects at length on our psychological, physiological and muscular responses to rhythms of various kinds, he offers no simplistic model of corporeal rhythms corresponding to regular verse. On the contrary, like the stars and the sea, the rhythms governing the human organism are a source of unanswerable questions:

The organism has its stopwatches and its metronomes. What are they? What time has it adopted? What pendulum beats?

These questions, if only we could answer them, would provide the thread and the most intimate link between the body and the cosmos from which it is separated. (*Cahiers*, 1916, VI, 278)

The young Parque, wrestling with the problematic experience of recognising a rhythmic pulse in herself, finds no solace in the regular beat of a 3/3/3/3 alexandrine:

> Mon cœur bat! / mon cœur bat! / Mon sein brûle / et m'entraîne! (27)
> (My heart beats! my heart beats! My breast burns and carries me away)

This regular rhythm provides no answers, nor any confirmation of the meaning of life. As the despairing Parque contemplates suicide, it is precisely the rhythmic part of herself which she intends to destroy: 'j'allai de mon cœur noyer les battements' (35) (I went to drown the beating of my heart); and as she contemplates death, her heart's faltering rhythm remains as mysterious as ever:

> Écoute, avec espoir, frapper au mur pieux
> Ce cœur, — qui se ruine à coups mystérieux (31)
> (Listen, with hope, as it knocks on the pious wall,
> To this heart, which ruins itself with mysterious beats)

Neither the stars, nor the sea, nor the human body, therefore, can provide a stable guarantee of a meaningful rhythm which pre-exists the text, and Valéry warns us to be sceptical of mimetic textual models of external rhythm. However, the creation and appreciation of artistic, literary or poetic structure is a profoundly human activity, and to deny inherently meaningful forms in nature is not to call for formlessness in art. Just as the human mind is predisposed to impose patterns, the interpretation of artistic structures, or the search for an interpretation, is a matter for the reader: 'Composition is the most *human* thing about the arts. Nature only offers systems at random; and we have to search for a link which establishes some relation between a whole and its parts. This requires man' (*Cahiers*, 1931, XIV: 808). Poetic rhythm, therefore, emerges as a constant search for an answer which, we must accept, can never be confirmed by any higher authority, and yet the urge to uncover the truth of this rhythm, the hope of an imminent revelation, remains.

Rhythm and composition

Given Valéry's dismissal of any extra-textual force producing rhythms for the poetic text to imitate, his insistent claims that several of his poems find their origin in some pre-textual rhythm may seem surprising:

It was born, like most of my poems, from the presence in my mind of a certain rhythm. I was astonished to find, one morning, decasyllabic lines in my head.[10]

As for the *Cimetière marin*, the intention was at first just an empty rhythmic figure, or filled with vain syllables, which came to obsess me for a while. I observed that this figure was decasyllabic. (Œ, I, 1503)

Another poem began in me by the simple indication of a rhythm which gave itself a meaning little by little. (Œ, I, 1474)

My poem *Le Cimetière marin* started in me with a certain rhythm, which is that of the French decasyllable, divided into four and six. I had no idea yet what should fill that form. (...) Another poem, *La Pythie*, first offered itself by a line of eight syllables whose sonority composed itself all on its own. (Œ, I, 1338)

As late as 1944, in the preface to his translation of Virgil's *Bucolics* into unrhymed alexandrines, Valéry maintains that it is the rhythm which comes first, and that a poet's 'internal work consists less of finding words for his ideas than of finding ideas for his words and predominant rhythms' (Œ, I, 212); similarly, as Emma Sutton observes in this volume, Virginia Woolf writes of 'putting words on the backs of rhythm'. We might be puzzled, then, by an apparent return to the idea of a rhythmic truth preceding the text. Yet in the above quotations, Valéry carefully situates the rhythm inside his own mind, not outside; furthermore, his is an extremely well-read mind familiar with the history of French verse forms, having spent many years grappling with the problems of composition. In this context, we might not be as surprised as he himself claims to be when he writes of composing almost unconsciously in metrical form: 'I was surprised to find myself versifying' (Œ, I, 1492). As such, poetic rhythm becomes a self-reflexive activity, reflecting only other textual models rather than a truth 'out there' in the world.

Such is Valéry's insistence on the role of a self-contained and self-perpetuating literary tradition in maintaining formal conventions, that he wonders whether anyone would invent verse had it not been bequeathed to them:

If literature had not existed before now — nor verse — would I have invented them? — Would our era have invented them? (*Cahiers*, 1917, VI, 566)

No-one would invent verse today, if it was not inherited. — Nor religions, for that matter. (*Cahiers*, 1926, XI, 410)

Perhaps not. Yet while he cuts all links between metrical verse and external guarantees, Valéry maintains there is a rhythmic instinct in man; a source of unanswerable questions it may be, but the organism responds to rhythms which correspond to certain vague structures within itself: 'A succession of noises is often taken for a rhythm but it is not quite a rhythm all on its own. It illuminates a rhythm in me' (*Cahiers*, 1914, V, 476). Explaining his return to poetry after twenty years (1892–1912), Valéry offers a newly heightened responsiveness to the sounds of language:

> I found myself becoming sensitive once more to what sounds in utterances. I
> lingered over perceiving the music of language. The words I heard set off in
> me I know not what harmonic dependences and implicit presence of imminent
> rhythms. (Œ, I, 1492)

Valéry is careful not to reduce linguistic music to the mere sounds of
words, but rather, to 'what sounds in utterances' (*ce qui sonne dans les
propos*). His renewed sensitivity is not simply to the form of language,
but rather, to the question of what it is, precisely, that we hear in
language beyond the semantic content, and how that corresponds
to the harmonic and rhythmic needs of the organism. Yet what,
exactly, are these harmonic dependences and imminent rhythms? And
what, precisely, is the nature of the 'utterances' which trigger his
response? Does he mean all examples of language, from conversation
to journalism, science, and literature, prose, and verse, or poetry read
aloud? Valéry writes expansively on the differences between prose
and poetry, and yet here, with uncharacteristic vagueness, it is the
sounds of indeterminate 'propos' which offer music to his ear. This
is a crucial question, since if language in its least literary incarnations
is already musical, rhythmic, harmonious, then there is no need for
poetry, indeed, poetry as a recognisable discourse disappears, since all
language is already poetry. There must be something, therefore, which
characterises poetic discourse as distinct from other utterances, and
while Valéry omits to state with any certainty what this mysterious
poetic quality is, it clearly has something to do with rhythm.

It is this sort of rhythmic instinct, Valéry suggests, that motivates
free verse poets: 'They deliberately break with conventions, and for
the cadences and musical substance of their verse, they rely on their
rhythmic instinct and their delicate ear alone' (Œ, I, 703). Similarly,
a poet's first draft represents 'the immediate record of his personal
rhythms, which are the form of his living energy system'.[11] Yet the
experience of these rhythms is always somehow problematic, and in
'La Création artistique' ('Artistic Creation'), Valéry gives a striking
example of a rhythm:

> which suddenly made itself very present in my mind, after a time during which
> I was only half-aware of this lateral activity. This rhythm imposed itself upon me,
> with a sort of insistence. (...) It seemed to me to want to take on a body, arrive at
> the perfection of being. But it could not become clearer to my consciousness
> without taking on some kind of *sayable* elements, syllables, words, and these

syllables and words were probably, at this point in the process, determined by their musical value and attractions. It was a draft stage, childish, where the form and the material can hardly be distinguished from each other, the rhythmic form providing at that point the only condition of admission, or emission. (*Vues*, 300)

Rhythm here appears as pure, pre-linguistic, unsayable (*indicible*); it requires formulating in words, in order to exist, in order for us to apprehend it, and yet that expression in words also veils it sufficiently to protect its absolute quality. The nature of poetic rhythm, therefore, lies in a kind of oscillation between an undefinable pre-textual absolute and textual forms which point to its existence beyond them; and since none of those textual forms can ever be an exact representation of the absolute literary rhythm, genuine poetic rhythm, in opposition to the mechanical, metrical and predictable, must be complex, shifting, elusive.

Rhythmic complexity

Valéry expresses this complex rhythmical model through the rhythms produced by footsteps, either in walking or dancing. Although the correspondence between verse and a fundamental rhythmic regularity in man is tempting — Crow, for example, claims that 'the voice of poetry, too, is made of measured treads, of heartbeats'[12] — Valéry carefully avoids this notion of 'measured treads', or simple ambulatory regularity. The only footsteps in his verse, as in these examples from *Charmes*, are complex, irregular, inexpressible, or forever held back on the cusp of a virtual movement:

> Les pas sidéraux ('Ode secrète', l.13)
> (The starry footsteps)
>
>   (. . .) des pas ineffables
> Qui marquent dans les fables ('Cantique des colonnes', ll.71–72)
>   (unsayable footsteps
> Which leave their mark in fables.)
>
> Personne pure, ombre divine,
> Qu'ils sont doux, tes pas retenus! ('Les Pas', ll.5–6)
> (Pure person, divine shadow,
> How sweet are your footsteps, held back!)

In the last example, the divine shadow of pure being does not walk, the poet preferring its footsteps when they remain pure potential, just as the homonym 'pas', the negator in French, cancels the verb which precedes it, and just as pure rhythm, which requires the impurity of words to embody it, can only remain pure on the brink of its expression in language.

References to footsteps in Valéry's *cahiers* develop this model of rhythmic complexity, such as this description of clambering down uneven rocks by the sea:

It is a dance, strange, because all the steps are different and none has the same amplitude or form as another; up, down, jumps, climbs, but a sort of rhythm remains (...) a dance whose steps' irregularity is the paradoxical law. (*Cahiers*, 1921, VIII, 224)

Eighteen years later, Valéry describes in detail a strange experience where the act of walking down a familiar street sets off a series of uncontrollable rhythmic connections of dizzying complexity:

As I walked along the street where I live, I was suddenly *seized* by a rhythm which imposed itself upon me, and which soon gave me the impression of working on me from outside. As if someone was using my *life machine*. Then another rhythm came to double the first and combine with it; and there established themselves I don't know what kind of *transversal* relationships between these two laws (I'm explaining it as best I can). This combined the walking movement of my legs with I know not what kind of song I was murmuring, or rather which murmured *through me*. This composition became more and more complicated, and soon became more complex than anything I could reasonably produce according to my ordinary, useable rhythmic faculties. Then the feeling of strangeness (...) became almost painful, almost worrying. I am not a musician; I am completely ignorant of musical technique; and here I was, prey to a development in several parts, more complicated than any poet could ever dream of. (Œ, I, 1322)

This rhythmical illumination then disappears as suddenly as it had arrived. In contrast to previous descriptions of metrical inspiration, which arise from the poet's own mind, here the rhythms seem to possess him from outside. What is most striking is Valéry's insistence on a complexity which surpasses his understanding, which can only be experienced bodily rather than with the analytical mind. This, rather than simple regular footsteps, appears to be the real human experience of rhythms for Valéry. Poetic rhythm may well respond to, or provoke, a fundamentally human experience — 'poetry must extend to the whole being; it arouses our muscular organisation through its rhythms' (Œ, I, 1394) — but nowhere does Valéry suggest that the experience of rhythm should be straightforward, regular, understandable. Rather, he tells us, 'there is a kind of pleasure which can be neither explained nor circumscribed' (*Œ*, I, 1311). It is on this undefinable, inexpressible, multiple rhythmic experience that poetry relies: 'it is almost only via rhythm and the sensory properties of language that literature can reach the organic being of a reader with any confidence in the conformity between the intention and the results' (*Vues*, 291).

The implications for verse analysis of this conception of poetic rhythm are far-reaching, especially in light of Valéry's professed aversion to formal analysis itself: 'I do not believe in analyses of French poetry based on rhythmics, etc' (*Cahiers*, 1929–30, XIV, 274); ten years later, he repeats his conviction that 'analyses of poetry through metrics, prosody, phonetics are quite insufficient' (*Cahiers*, 1940, XXIII, 197). Valéry thus strongly counters the Parnassian belief that poeticity may be quantified formally: 'Try as we might to count the steps of the goddess, to note their frequency and *average* length, it will not teach us the secret of her instantaneous grace' (*Œ*, I, 1285). Beauty may only now be defined as 'this uncertainty which confounds all calculations' (*Œ*, I, 1287); indeed, 'to say that an object is *beautiful* is to give it the value of an enigma' (*Œ*, I, 1301). It is the role of poetic rhythm, therefore, to preserve that mystery by simultaneously pointing towards, and holding back from, its imminent revelation, since 'Legs are not only for getting across and arriving—and words are not only for learning or teaching' (*Cahiers*, 1916, VI, 182).

While rhythm, then, survives the *crise de vers* as a vehicle for both experiencing and thinking poeticity, it acquires a new complexity and becomes so central to poetic discourse that, even in the absence of an external mimetic model, we are invited to imagine that it somehow exists beyond the text. Valéry argues that rhythmically and structurally complex verse actually creates the illusion of having sprung from real life, not unlike his strange experience of walking previously quoted:

Verse is that language in which the sonority and the linking of words, their signifying effect and their psychological resonances, the rhythms, the syntactic arrangements are so tightly bound that our memory is necessarily cleansed of them, and the words form an object which appears as if it were *natural*, as if it were born out of real life. (*Cahiers*, 1922, VIII, 586)

The important words here are 'as if' (*comme*). The complex, multiple and artificial structures of verse may at certain privileged moments appear to correspond to external rhythmical truths, indeed, it is the peculiar power of poetry to provoke precisely that illusion, but it remains an illusion nonetheless. Valéry describes himself succumbing to the same illusion in music: 'Beautiful music, you inspire my hatred and my desire. I know that you lie, and yet I follow you. You pretend to know, to hold — you recreate, you form and reform — and I know that you do not know and that you move us as if you led to the secret' (*Cahiers*, 1907–08, IV, 354). In an article which asks 'how to put prosody back at the centre of the way in which we think about poems and poetry (...) how to understand prosody's elusive yet undeniable cognitive character', Simon Jarvis draws a similar conclusion: 'it is hard to escape the implication that there is something constitutively illusory about what it is that music attempts to express'.[13] In an early letter to Gide, Valéry observes the same process in poetry: 'I have read the most marvellous Poe, Rimbaud, Mallarmé, analysed, alas, their methods, and each time I have come across the most beautiful illusions' (11891).[14] It is this illusion, nurtured by poetry itself — that rhythm does exist out there — that we, as readers of poetry, are conditioned into accepting; Valéry is clearer than anyone on how this rhythmic illusion functions, and by placing a post-illusory formalism at the heart of his poetics, provides something like the 'kind of idealism — a sober, non-metaphysical, indeed an anti-metaphysical, almost, it may be thought, a *materialist* kind of idealism' upon which Jarvis's study concludes.[15]

Rhythm as deferral

Thanks to its rhythmic complexity and structural multiplicity, verse, for Valéry, can never be exhausted in the reading: 'A beautiful line of verse is reborn indefinitely from its ashes' (Œ, I, 1510), a 1929 formula which he takes up ten years later: 'the poem does not die for having lived: it is made expressly to be reborn from its ashes' (Œ, I, 1331). This recalls Derrida's understanding of writing, as Peter Dayan puts it: 'Like music, writing cannot be said to arrive, it cannot reach us, cannot happen (...) but unlike music, as a thing, as a form, its duty is to be consumed, to vanish, to leave behind it only ashes'.[16] Only unanalysable form, the kind to which Valéry's intricate verse structures aspire, can allow the text to be reborn from the ashes of the reading, and crucially, for Derrida, that capacity to escape fixity constantly is expressed as rhythm: 'As it escapes from all forms that writing can determine, it acquires the force of rhythm (...) not analysable rhythm, not representable form, but a kind of rhythm which always escapes, and must always be re-thought, re-invented, re-imagined'.[17] Unlike prose which, Valéry often argues, exists to take the reader from A to B, with B representing the final term to be understood, the rhythmic fabric of verse enacts formally the fundamental impossibility of concluding, since 'if everything were deciphered, everything would disappear instantaneously' (Œ, II, 506). Indeed, for Valéry, the essence of poetry is a resistance to closure, a constant hesitation:

> The poetic idea (...) a clear ambiguity, presenting in a fragment, on a given point, the resonance of the whole being. (*Cahiers*, 1915, V, 637)

> The poet's business is to construct a sort of verbal body which might have the solidity, but the ambiguity, of an object. (*Cahiers*, 1916, VI, 118)

> Ambiguity is the rightful domain of poetry. (*Cahiers*, 1916, VI, 343)

> This *state of poetry* is perfectly irregular, inconstant, involuntary, fragile. (Œ, I, 1321)

Whoever looks for one single, fixed truth in 'la forêt enchantée du Langage' (the enchanted forest of Language), Valéry explains, is doomed to disappointment:

> The huntsman who gets worked up chasing the 'truth', following a single, continuous path, of which each element is the only one he must take, for fear of losing the path or the gains of the road hitherto travelled, risks capturing only his/its shadow. Gigantic, sometimes; but a shadow nonetheless. (Œ, I, 1300–01)

In a typically Mallarmean piece of sleight of hand, it is unclear from the French what the possessive in 'ne capturer enfin que son ombre' refers to; does the truth-seeker find a shadow of the truth he was searching for, or a shadow of himself? Is the truth in art an internal, human truth, or does it exist out there, in language, in the universe? Surely, as we have seen, that ambiguity is central to poetry, and it is rhythm which helps the poet maintain this quintessentially poetic hesitation, fuelling but never satisfying our 'need to find a suitable definition of poetry, at the very least a decisive characteristic — and this need itself is born of our inability to discover the real poetic principle' (*Cahiers*, 1918, VII, 71).

It is in rhythm that Valéry locates the universally human response to poetry, a rhythm which provides no answers, which resists definition, and yet which, in its mystery and complexity, represents the truth of both the human condition and the poetic enterprise: 'Why not admit that man is the source, the origin of enigmas, since there is no object, no being, no instant which is not impenetrable' (*Œ*, I, 650). Just as Mallarmé's famously mysterious 'obscure' poems work by '*making you expect and desire* some resolution' (*Cahiers*, 1940–41, XXIV, 150) and yet by constantly deferring it, Valéry's theory of rhythm establishes a sense of familiarity, or recognition, a desire for resolution, and yet its complexity resists our understanding, allowing verse to be born again with every reading. As Robert Pickering observes, 'rhythm, for Valéry, is a concept in a state of perpetual becoming'.[18] Moreover, it is a state which both needs language in which to manifest itself, and yet rejects it, providing its own sort of truth, a state which approaches that imagined by Simon Jarvis: 'If we can imagine forms of thinking and knowing which are not linguistic, and which do not rest upon linguistic modes of making-explicit, then we are also in that act imagining meanings and ways of meaning which are not like the relation of a signifier to a signified'.[19] Rhythm, then, is always in process, never fixed; always mobile, unstable; it provides no clear answers, but rather, provokes unanswerable questions, and it is this elusive, challenging, unsettling characteristic which ensures rhythm remains central to twentieth-century poetry and its exploration of what it means to be human and in the world, teasing us with the promise of answers which it perpetually defers.

NOTES

1   Valéry's italics. The italics in all quotations are Valéry's own. References to Valéry's prose are from *Œuvres*, edited by Jean Hytier (Paris: Gallimard, coll. 'Bibliothèque de la Pléiade', 1957) and *Ego scriptor*, edited by Judith Robinson-Valéry (Paris: Gallimard, coll. 'Poésie', 1992), which contains selections from his *Cahiers* in chronological order. French verse will be given in the original with accompanying translation, while prose will be given in English only, unless commented on at the level of the signifier. All translations are my own.

2   See Benoît de Cornulier, *Théorie du vers* (Paris: Seuil, 1982), 133–44 for an explanation of the various types of caesural infringement.

3   Letter to Jacques Doucet, 1922, quoted in Brian Stimpson, *Paul Valéry and Music* (Cambridge: Cambridge University Press, 1984), 175.

4   In another striking parallel with Emma Sutton's opening quotation, this echoes Woolf's suggestion that the writer has not to fix rhythm in the text, but rather to set it working.

5   One of the strengths of Henri Meschonnic's *Critique du Rythme* (Lagrasse: Verdier, 1982) is its similarly staunch refusal to see poetic rhythm as a mimesis of cosmic or bodily rhythms; see the sections entitled 'L'imitation cosmique' (617–42) and 'Critique de l'anthropologie du rythme' (643–702).

6   Victor Hugo, *Les Contemplations* (Paris: Gallimard, 1973), 376.

7   Walter Ince, 'Some of Valéry's reflections on rhythm', in *Baudelaire, Mallarmé, Valéry: New Essays in Honour of Lloyd James Austin*, edited by Malcolm Bowie, Alison Fairlie and Alison Finch (Cambridge: Cambridge University Press, 1982), 384–97 (395) and Christine Crow, *Paul Valéry and the Poetry of Voice* (Cambridge: Cambridge University Press, 1982), 83.

8   Hugo, *Océan. Faits et croyances*, in *Œuvres complètes*, 18 vols, edited by Jean Massin (Paris: Le Club Français du Livre, 1967–70), VII, 700.

9   *La Jeune Parque* (Paris, Gallimard, 1974), 17.

10 Frédéric Lefèvre, *Entretiens avec Paul Valéry* (Paris: Le Livre, 1926), 62.

11 'Comment travaillent les écrivains', *Vues* (Paris, La Tables Ronde, 1948), 317.

12 *Paul Valéry and the Poetry of Voice*, 149.

13 'Musical Thinking: Hegel and the Phenomenology of Prosody', *Paragraph* 28 : 2 (July 2005), 57–71 (57 and 65).

14 1891, *Gide-Valéry Correspondance* (Paris, 1955), 126.

15 'Musical Thinking', 69; Jarvis's italics.

16 'Derrida Writing Architectural or Musical Form', *Paragraph* 26:3 (November 2003), 70–85 (83).

17 'Derrida Writing Architectural or Musical Form', 82.

18 '"Tes pas... procèdent": melos, marche, méditation dans les promenades de Rousseau et de Valéry', in *Paul Valéry: Musique, mystique, mathématique*, edited by Paul Gifford and Brian Stimpson (Lille: Presses Universitaires de Lille, 1993), 95–112.

19 'Musical Thinking', 69.

'Putting Words on the Backs of Rhythm': Woolf, 'Street Music', and *The Voyage Out*[1]

EMMA SUTTON

Abstract:

This essay explores Virginia Woolf's representation of rhythm in two early texts — her neglected 1905 essay 'Street Music' and her first novel, *The Voyage Out* (1915). It teases out the texts' characterisations of musical, literary, bodily and urban rhythms, considering their implications for a theory of literary rhythm more broadly. Arguing that rhythm has a central place in Woolf's writing practice, prose style and theories of writing, the essay charts the relationship between rhythm, individuality and literary value in these texts, and in selected correspondence, diary extracts, essays and fiction.

Keywords: rhythm, Virginia Woolf, 'Street Music', *The Voyage Out*, literary-musical relations, primitivism

As for the mot juste, *you are quite wrong. Style is a very simple matter; it is all rhythm. Once you get that, you can't use the wrong words. But on the other hand here am I sitting after half the morning, crammed with ideas, and visions, and so on, and can't dislodge them, for lack of the right rhythm. Now this is very profound, what rhythm is, and goes far deeper than words. A sight, an emotion, creates this wave in the mind, long before it makes words to fit it; and in writing (such is my present belief) one has to recapture this, and set this working (which has nothing apparently to do with words) and then, as it breaks and tumbles in the mind, it makes words to fit it . . .*

Letter to Vita Sackville-West, March 1926.

All writing is nothing but putting words on the backs of rhythm. If they fall off the rhythm one's done . . .

Letter to Ethel Smyth, April 1931.[2]

Virginia Woolf's pithy observation to the composer Ethel Smyth defines 'writing' entirely in terms of rhythm. 'Nothing' else matters, whether we understand the term 'writing' in its most immediate sense as the process of composition or, as Woolf's phrasing also permits, as a corpus of texts. Here, a writer's rhythmic sense determines the

Paragraph 33:2 (2010) 176–196
DOI: 10.3366/E0264833410000830

success of 'all writing'; it is not only a matter of 'style', as her earlier observations to Sackville-West suggest, but of literary value *in toto*. Her absolute language implies that rhythm's centrality to writing is undeniable, yet the absence of any explanatory detail to Smyth hints too that it is difficult to define with precision. Writing to Sackville-West, Woolf characterises her theory as provisional, acknowledging that to speak of rhythm is both problematic and 'profound': her frequent reaching for metaphor evokes the inadequacy of critical vocabulary to elucidate this aspect of prose.[3] These observations centralize but complicate rhythm's role in (her own) writing, exemplifying Woolf's enduring attention to but elusive, sometimes deceptively casual, theoretical conceptions of literary rhythm. Woolf makes the statement to Smyth apparently spontaneously, for example, following an apology for the 'drivvle' [*sic*] of her letter, which she attributes in part to the effects of 'the loudspeaker (...) pouring forth Wagner from Paris.' The German composer's rhythm 'destroys' hers, she tells Smyth, adding, 'yes, thats [*sic*] a true observation.'[4] So her seemingly impulsive remarks about rhythm are given weight and emphasis by Woolf's claim about the 'truth' of her observations, just as the earlier observations to Vita Sackville-West are both considered and simply a reply to an unanticipated assertion of Vita's.

Woolf's observations appear conversational, but their implications for a theory of rhythm are complex. Woolf's implied metaphor to Smyth is presumably of rhythm as the horse(s) on which 'words', the riders, sit.[5] Her image characterizes rhythm as animated, purposeful and autonomous; it predates and determines the choice of words 'put' on it, just as, in the letter to Vita, rhythm 'makes words to fit it'. Rhythm is primary whilst words are secondary — fragile and unstable, prone to 'fall[ing] off'. Rhythm, implicitly, has a generative and epistemological force; as Woolf reiterates elsewhere, 'meaning' is not constructed only by 'words'. In these accounts, rhythm precedes the act of 'writing', though whether it is perceived to exist externally or internally, in the writer's creative mind or body, varies in Woolf's accounts. The implied allusion to horses, like that to waves 'break[ing]' and 'tumbl[ing]', does associate rhythm with the natural world (albeit a partially domesticated version of nature), but this is not to say that Woolf's image necessarily suggests a single cosmic rhythm or, indeed, 'natural' rhythms determined by the gender, race or sexuality of the writer. Rather, her unexpected use of the plural ('backs', rather than 'back') suggests that rhythm is varied and multiple: it varies by individual ('[Wagner's] rhythm', 'my rhythm') and by text (in 1940, she 'br[eaks]' 'up' the 'obsessive' rhythm of one text by reading another).[6] Successful or 'literary' rhythm is individual, non-uniform, it 'breaks' and 'tumbles', disrupting the apparent sameness of the waves.[7] Both images suggest the potential, and the necessity, for literary rhythm to unsettle, exceed or otherwise escape the semblance of order and regularity represented by the waves and the riders. The plural also allows the possibility that rhythm may also refer to culturally specific, historically determined, rather than natural rhythms — the diverse rhythmic and metrical conventions of literature or music, for example.[8] Thus, although the equine and sea images unequivocally associate rhythm with the natural world, Woolf variously imagines rhythm as natural or corporeal, aesthetic and historically specific, or both. The very possibility that rhythm may escape the control of its rider evokes its resistance to definition.

These two epigraphs exemplify the complexity of Woolf's conceptions of rhythm, which occupies a privileged place in her prose style, writing practice, and theories of writing. Accounts of Woolf drafting her prose aloud as she walked are well known[9] and many have noted the distinctive rhythms of Woolf's prose, particularly the late fiction, though the term itself has rarely been explored in detail.[10] And the fiction itself frequently explores the properties and effects of musical, urban and spoken rhythms — the waltz to which Sara listens in the 1907 section of *The Years* (1937) and the disjointed colloquial speech of *Between the Acts* (1941) are obvious examples. Feminist readings of the rhythms of Woolf's prose have recently been augmented by scholarship on her representations of the voice and acoustic experience more generally, and by the influence of musical forms on her fiction;[11] to many, Woolf's own prose anticipates, and is a productive site for encounters with, the theoretical turn to the aural evident in the work of Kristeva, Cixous, Jean-Luc Nancy and others. The 'crise de vers' (crisis in verse) is thus one among a number of discourses and texts shaping Woolf's interest in and theories of rhythm. Though the present essay is not primarily concerned with questions of 'influence', it is probable that Woolf knew of the arguments comprising the 'crise de vers' and possibly Mallarmé's essay specifically. She alluded intermittently to Mallarmé in her letters and essays from the 1920s onwards,[12] and may have read his work in French well before this date. Her remarks in 1920 to Roger Fry about his planned translation of selected poems confirm, for example, that she already knew these texts well[13] (and when Fry's translations were posthumously published in 1936 she described them as 'a masterpiece').[14] Her familiarity with Mallarmé's work provides a further context in which to consider Woolf's observations on rhythm, placing her work in relation to late nineteenth-century discourses about rhythm, music and literary meaning or value. Thus, my attention here is not to the influence of specific musical forms or genres on her writing, but to the way Woolf represents the relationship between musical and literary rhythm and deploys the persistent, elusive analogy between music, literature and rhythm.

There has been little critical attention to the representation of rhythm in Woolf's early fiction, even though it was in this period that Woolf published two essays on music and her most explicit theorization of literary and musical rhythm, 'Street Music' (1905). Preceding Woolf's longer and more famous commentaries on contemporary writing (such as 'Modern Novels' (1919), and 'Mr Bennett and Mrs Brown' (1924)) by some years, 'Street Music' centralizes rhythm in her analysis of prose. Her first novel, *The Voyage Out* (1915), was begun within three years of this essay and traces the amateur pianist Rachel Vinrace's voyage to South America and her eventual engagement to a novelist, Terence Hewet.[15] I aim here to animate the relations between these two texts: the first, her most extended theorization of rhythm, the second, her first novel which also deals prominently with literary-musical relations. The novel includes many conversations about literary-musical relations and the nature of Art, yet rhythm plays a small part in these discussions. Nonetheless, the text refers repeatedly and conspicuously to different types, effects and uses of rhythm. At the very start of the novel, Woolf employs incompatible affective rhythms to convey the characters' relations and interior lives. Helen Ambrose's distress at leaving her children is exacerbated by her husband's chanting of Macaulay's *Lays of Ancient Rome* (1842): Macaulay's ballad 'struck close upon her ears', and she finds Ridley's 'quick rhythmic stride' and subsequent self-identification with masculine heroes such as 'a Viking or a stricken Nelson' uncongenial.[16] Her rhythmic weeping and 'fixity of mood' are, however, 'broken by the action of walking' and by the accompanying sounds of 'thundering drays' and 'jingling hansoms' (5). From the opening of the text, and throughout, Woolf suggests that rhythm — poetic, urban or bodily — is constitutive and expressive of subjectivity.[17] Furthermore, prose rhythms, poetic metre and music are contrasted throughout *The Voyage Out*. The present essay has a modest aim: rather than attempting to characterize the rhythm(s) of Woolf's prose in *The Voyage Out*, it offers some preliminary observations on her *representation* of metre and rhythm in 'Street Music' and in the novel, teasing out the theoretical implications of her conceptions of rhythm. There is, I will suggest, a sharp contrast between the utopian argument of 'Street Music' and her uneasy representation of literary rhythm in *The Voyage Out*.

Unlike Woolf's essays on art music ('The Opera' and 'Impressions at Bayreuth', both 1909), 'Street Music' examines rhythm explicitly and at some length.[18] The essay's relative neglect is surprising given Woolf's famous later statements about rhythm;[19] possibly, it has been perceived as a period piece partly because the representation of rhythm is, at first glance, resoundingly primitivist. The essay begins with three paragraphs on 'vagrant musician[s]' (27), delineating the 'ecstasy' of an old violinist before criticizing the English 'disfavour' towards musicians and artists more generally, an attitude attributed to a national perception of 'expression of any kind' as 'almost indecent' and 'unmanly' (28). The first-person narrator notes that musicians are 'persecute[d]' (29): 'It is because music incites within us something that is wild and inhuman like itself — a spirit that we would willingly stamp out and forget — that we are distrustful of musicians and loath to put ourselves under their power' (29). The reference to stamping hints that rhythm is this problematic element in music and this implication is expanded as the essay continues. Should the 'pagan gods' exiled under Christianity return, it 'will be the god of music who will breathe madness into our brains, crack the walls of our temples, and drive us in loathing of our rhythmless [*sic*] lives to dance and circle for ever in obedience to his voice' (30). This sentence introduces the explicit discussion, rather than only the evocation, of rhythm, and this subject occupies the remaining half of the essay. The narrator criticizes contemporary music education, which is associated with the feminine domestic accomplishments of flower pressing and piano playing:

The whole of rhythm and harmony have been pressed, like dried flowers, into the neatly divided scales, the tones and semitones of the pianoforte. The safest and easiest attribute of music — its tune — is taught, but rhythm, which is its soul, is allowed to escape like the winged creature it is. (30)

Woolf's image modifies her evocation of the corporeality of rhythm, evoked by dance: now, rhythm has become ethereal, a 'winged creature' and a 'soul' — and thus, in true Mallarmean fashion, endowed with spiritual value which exceeds or escapes that which can be taught or 'neatly divided'. As in her later image of rhythm as horses, rhythm again escapes definition or theorization. The essay asserts too that the uneducated and 'savages' — 'whose sense of rhythm has never been divorced [sic] or made subsidiary to their sense of tune' (30) — are most sensitive to rhythm:

The beat of rhythm in the mind is akin to the beat of the pulse in the body: and thus though many are deaf to tune hardly anyone is so coarsely organised as not to hear the rhythm of its own heart in words and music and movement. It is because it is thus inborn in us that we can never silence music, any more than we can stop our heart from beating; and it is for this reason too that music is so universal and has the strange and illimitable power of a natural force. (30)

Woolf's definition keeps ambivalent possibilities in play: rhythm is everywhere and nowhere, 'universal' yet always escaping, corporeal and 'inborn' yet ethereal and the locus of spiritual value, 'akin to' yet also directly equated with the 'heart' and 'pulse'. Furthermore, if rhythm had seemed the vigorous 'masculine' property of music that escaped feminized amateur domestic music education (or, had rhythm rather been gendered female by its ethereality?), Woolf is now careful to use neutral language in the grammatically awkward phrase 'its own heart'. Rhythm is both male and female (or neither) — perhaps analogous to the androgynous creative mind evoked in *A Room of One's Own* by the 'rhythmical order' of the 'ordinary sight' of a man and a woman getting into a cab?[20] Having asserted music's 'power over us' (30), the narrator goes on to consider the 'strange sight' (30) of a room of dancers: 'it may be that some day it will suggest the vast possibilities that lie within the power of rhythm, and the whole of our life will be revolutionised as it was when man first realised the power of steam' (31). The remainder of the essay sketches the social and aesthetic benefits that would result if 'the affairs of daily life' were 'order[ed]' to a 'sense of rhythm' (31). From road rage, Woolf moves to social relations and crime:

a band in the centre of the wild discord of cabs and carriages would be more effectual than any policeman; not only cabman but horse would find himself constrained to keep time in the dance, and to follow whatever measure of trot or canter the trumpets dictated. This principle has been in some degree recognised in the army, where troops are inspired to march into battle to the rhythm of music. (...) Conversation, for instance, would not only obey its proper laws of metre as dictated by our sense of rhythm, but would be inspired by charity, love and wisdom, and ill-temper or sarcasm would sound to the bodily ear as terrible discords and false notes. (...) If, therefore, instead of libraries, philanthropists would bestow free music upon the poor, so that at each street corner the melodies of Beethoven and Brahms and Mozart could be heard, it is probable that all crime and quarrelling would soon be unknown, and the work of the hand and the thoughts of the mind would flow melodiously in obedience to the laws of music. (31–2)

The essay concludes with the anticipation that 'our lives would pass from dawn to sunset to the sound of music' (32).

As these examples suggest, the essay's apparent celebration of rhythm is substantially qualified by Woolf's unstable tone, which oscillates between Romantic primitivism and irony. (The editor for whom she wrote the piece described it as a 'paradox', and Woolf wrote wryly to her cousin Emma Vaughan, studying music in Dresden, that her essay would 'revolutionise the whole future of music').[21] The essay's utopian visions of individuals and society reformed by rhythm so that conversations are conducted along the Pauline virtues of 'charity, love and wisdom' become steadily more hyperbolic, incongruously Christian, and psychologically and politically naïve. The increasingly bold claims in 'Street Music' about rhythm's socio-political agency are qualified by their overstatement and by the juxtaposition of brief, unsupported examples. Woolf's allusion to military uses of rhythm also immediately signals the ambivalence of these utopian visions: as she would later do in *The Voyage Out*, Woolf associates military rhythm with patriarchal aggression, undercutting the essay's apparent argument. The allusions to 'troops', 'cabm[e]n' and 'policem[e]n' hint, perhaps, that stably gendered rhythm that relies on an inflexible binary conception of gender is the antithesis of the 'literary' rhythm for which the essay appeals.[22] The benevolent social effects of rhythm are further compromised if we recall that the argument and examples of the essay are anticipated in a letter of 1903, in which she described the Stephen family's experiments in using the pianola as a form of social control:[23]

our servants sit beneath the open drawing room window all the evening while we play — and by experiment we have discovered that if we play dance music all their crossnesses [*sic*] vanish and the whole room rings with their shrieks and then we tame them down so sentimentally with Saul or [*sic*] boredom with Schumann — on the whole their silence is the most desirable thing.[24]

The self-interest knowingly admitted in the letter, as well as the silencing of the animalistic servants, suggest Woolf's alertness to the class politics embedded in the essay's similar depiction of rhythm (where 'the poor' will be the subjects of rhythmic experimentation).[25] All of these factors suggest the essay's ambivalence towards primitivism and towards the concept of a single universal rhythm, whether that of the 'heart' and 'pulse' (30) or of nature, whose 'vast pulsation' can be detected in forests (31). The essay is, then, ambivalent about rhythm, which is variously imagined as individualistic, disruptive and ecstatic or as regular, militaristic, and socially coercive. This dialectical model recurs in Woolf's later representations of rhythm, in which 'literary' rhythm is often defined by contrast with its opposite; frequently, 'literary' rhythm is represented as the ideal — in the sense both that it is abstract, resistant to one single definition, and that it is celebrated for its individualism and difference. The essay's variable tone itself signals Woolf's privileging of instability and disruption over the utilitarian, mechanistic conception of regular rhythm.

How, then, are we to read the essay's assertion that literature is the closest art to music, and thus to rhythm? The narrator argues that 'the art of writing' should be reformed by the influence of rhythm (note the proximity, even synonymity, of art and rhythm again). Furthermore, the essay insists that contemporary writing will derive its originality and aesthetic value from rhythm:

And when the sense of rhythm was thoroughly alive in every mind we should if I mistake not, [*sic*] notice a great improvement not only in the ordering of all the affairs of daily life, but also in the art of writing, which is nearly allied to the art of music, and is chiefly degenerate because it has forgotten its allegiance. We should invent — or rather remember — the innumerable metres which we have so long outraged, and which would restore both prose and poetry to the harmonies that the ancients heard and observed. (31)

Woolf's essay has, albeit ironically, elements of a manifesto for modern writing — though it is a vision of modern writing that, like those of many modernists, looks back to nineteenth-century perceptions of music's potential to exceed the expressivity of language.[26] 'Street Music' identifies 'music' and 'ancient' metres as the models for modern literary rhythms, and at this point Woolf defines rhythm primarily in relation to aesthetic history and the 'mind' rather than to the 'bodily ear' or cosmic rhythm (though the 'harmony of the spheres' is also evoked in the final phrase). She seems, that is, to be about to supply a more specific definition of rhythm. Yet Woolf avoids explicitly identifying the literary and musical genres, forms, and even cultural or historical contexts of these rhythmic models. Her reference to 'metres' may, in conjunction with the classical allusions in the essay, suggest that she is referring to the sung texts of classical Greek poetry; Woolf was certainly very familiar not only with classical Greek metre and theories of 'rhythmopoeia' or 'rhythmic composition' but also with the interdependence of musical and literary rhythms in Greek poetry.[27] However, the 'ancient' 'metres' may suggest Latin or even Hebrew metres to some readers, and it is, in any case, unclear how literally we should — or could — take Woolf's invitation. In addition to the critical disagreement about the exact sounds of these ancient metres, the great majority of readers, as Woolf knew very well, can have had no precise sense of the sounds and rhythms to which she was alluding.[28] How, then, can they 'remember' them? These are, for all practical purposes, unheard metres: the rhythms remain, therefore, essentially abstract and metaphorical.[29] Rhythm simultaneously defines the literary value of modern(ist) writing—including, presumably, Woolf's own prose—and evades definition.

In contrast to 'Street Music', which asserts the affinity between musical and literary rhythm and looks to music and sung poetic metre to reinvigorate modern writing, *The Voyage Out* sharply contrasts the properties and effects of musical and literary rhythms. Woolf's numerous representations of characters reading or declaiming poetry and prose establish the problematic effects of poetic metre and literary rhythm more generally. Repeatedly, Woolf depicts the rhythm of canonical literary texts by male authors in extreme terms—as troublingly affective, soporific or as obfuscating meaning. Among the numerous literary allusions, there are several prominent references to Gibbon; St John praises his style and recommends him to the uneducated Rachel. The first extended representation of St John describes him reading the *History of the Decline and Fall of the Roman Empire* (1776–88); it is, implicitly, the rhythm of Gibbon's prose, evoked by the rhythmic tapping of his cigarette, by which St John is absorbed:

As he read he knocked the ash automatically, now and again, from his cigarette and turned the page, while a whole procession of splendid sentences entered his capacious brow and went marching through his brain in order. It seemed likely that this process might continue for an hour or more, until the entire regiment had shifted its quarters, had not the door opened (...). (116)

Compare Rachel's first reading of the text:

Never had any words been so vivid and so beautiful — Arabia Felix — Aethiopia. But those were not more noble than the others, hardy barbarians, forests, and morasses. They seemed to drive roads back to the very beginning of the world, on either side of which the populations of all times and countries stood in avenues, and by passing down them all knowledge would be hers, and the book of the world turned back to the very first page. Such was her excitement at the possibilities of knowledge now opening before her that she ceased to read (...). (196)

The explicitly rhythmic and martial image of a military 'procession' 'marching' as St John reads is inflected in Rachel's hint of colonial expansion where the 'populations of all times and countries st[and] in avenues' as roads are 'drive[n] back' (a reading encouraged by the novel's setting in a fictional South American colonial resort). However, Woolf attributes her characters' differing responses to their ability to 'hear' Gibbon's rhythm. St John is arrested by the sound of Gibbon's prose (the regular beat of marching) whilst Rachel's response is to individual 'words' rather than to repetitive sound — and the words' 'vivid[ness]' which, as the *Oxford English Dictionary* notes, is a term frequently used 'of light or colour', suggests perhaps that Rachel's attention is as much to the words' visual as their aural associations. Woolf emphasizes Rachel's excitement and pleasure at this symbolic introduction to the patriarchal canon — yet, crucially, she stops reading, interrupting or breaking the rhythm of the prose. Whereas Gibbon's rhythm appears tenacious and 'order[ly]' to St John, it has no such power to regulate or sustain Rachel's reading; indeed, she later observes that it 'goes round, round, round, like a roll of oilcloth', though she is 'instantly ashamed of her figure of speech, for she could not explain it in words of sober criticism' (226). Rachel's scathing caricature of Gibbon's rhythm suggests the uncongeniality of his prose style — in *A Room of One's Own*, Gibbon exemplifies the 'man's sentence' 'current at the beginning of the nineteenth century', 'unsuited for a woman's use'.[30] The episode records Rachel's pleasure, but also implicitly questions Gibbon's relevance to her and, by extension, to the contemporary woman artist. Rachel may lack critical vocabulary, and rhythm itself resists 'sober criticism', but her ear for rhythm allows her to identify immediately the very features of Gibbon's style by which St John was absorbed. And as we will see when we return to Rachel' musical performance, it is rhythmic regularity and repetition that repel her.

It is in the novel's depictions of poetry, however, that Woolf diverges furthest from the celebration of literary rhythm and metre in 'Street Music.' In the novel, regular poetic metre is repeatedly associated with characters' distress, illness and even death, and this characteristic becomes increasingly marked as Rachel's illness develops.

When Rachel is taken ill with the fever that will kill her, her fiancé Terence is reading *Comus* (1634):

> It was too hot to talk, and it was not easy to find any book that would withstand the power of the sun. Many books had been tried and then let fall, and now Terence was reading Milton aloud, because he said the words of Milton had substance and shape, so that it was not necessary to understand what he was saying; one could merely listen to his words; one could almost handle them. (...) The words, in spite of what Terence had said, seemed to be laden with meaning, and perhaps it was for this reason that it was painful to listen to them; they sounded strange; they meant different things from what they usually meant. Rachel at any rate could not keep her attention fixed upon them, but went off upon curious trains of thought suggested by words such as 'curb' and 'Locrine' and 'Brute', which brought unpleasant sights before her eyes, independently of their meaning. (380–81)

The diegetic declamation of Milton's masque and Terence's invitation to 'merely listen' emphasize the aural aspects of the text and of the characters' experience. Despite their different perceptions of Milton's language, both Terence and Rachel appear to believe that sound, perhaps more specifically rhythm, conveys its own 'meaning'.[31] Certainly, 'understand[ing]' and value are not dependent on rational comprehension or even semiotic stability (the words 'meant different things'); aesthetic pleasure and comprehension may come by 'merely listen[ing]' — even if 'listen[ing]' has less apparent critical authority than 'understand[ing]'. Rhythmic appreciation differs, this suggests, from the critical or perhaps even the semantic, and the passage implicitly invites us as readers to engage in this alternative form of understanding. This experience is, however, sinister rather than comic and this is due, I would suggest, to the fact that this part of the masque is set to, and is about, music. The passage that Terence quotes is the Attendant Spirit's description of, and the opening lines of his song to, Sabrina; the Spirit is imploring Sabrina's help for the Lady and his successful summoning of the 'gentle nymph' (380) depends on the beauty of his 'warbled song'.[32] Woolf quotes and emphasises the stressed imperatives of the song in which the Spirit repeatedly instructs Sabrina to 'listen': 'Sabrina fair, / Listen where thou art sitting', 'Listen for dear honour's sake', 'Listen and save!' (381). The repetition of 'listen' underlines not only the aural but also the musical qualities of Milton's verse, drawing our attention to the fact that this part of the masque is (or could be) sung rather than spoken.[33] This section of the masque is thus not only *about* the affective agency of music and sung poetry, but also is a form of writing (a 'song') intended to accompany music (written for the first performance by Henry Lawes, the court musician). Its composition and performance are thus intrinsically associated with music, so we might expect that this would be an appealing neo-classical variant of the 'ancient' metres evoked in 'Street Music', an appealing example of musical-literary 'allegiance'. Clearly, this is not the case. Rather, the words 'sound strange' to Rachel, and the first day of her delirium is occupied with 'try[ing] to remember how the lines [of the song] went' (383): 'the effort worried her because the adjectives persisted in getting in to the wrong places' (384). Syntax has become unstable, but Rachel retains a grasp on the sound and rhythm of Milton's verse (rather, perhaps, it retains a grasp on her). Woolf represents Rachel's illness in further images of rhythmic disturbance and silence: the violent 'pulse' of her headache signals the start of her fever (382), whilst its progression is marked by the sudden cessation of 'the song that someone was singing in the garden' (383) and her increasing isolation from the 'sounds' of the 'outer world' (384). There are several reasons why Milton's words may be 'painful' (the drowning of the young virgin Sabrina, for instance, prefigures the aquatic imagery of Rachel's own death) but the allusions to Rachel's 'pulse', and the repetitive echoing of 'listen', suggests that it is the regularity of this rhythm that is problematic. Milton's 'song' appears not only affective but also sinister, a disturbing antithesis to the beneficial 'musical' and literary metres sketched in 'Street Music'.

When Rachel's illness is in its final stages, repetitive poetic metre again provides a painful and unwelcome intrusion into the characters' subjectivities. Ridley quotes Charles Kingsley's 'A New Forest Ballad' (1847); as with *Comus*, the choice of text prefigures the sudden death of a youth and Ridley quotes the lines immediately before the murders occur. As the narrator describes Ridley's behaviour, their voice anticipates the internal rhymes, alliteration and repetition of Kingsley's ballad, highlighting the marked, repetitive rhythm of his text:

the sound of Ridley's song and the beat of his pacing worked into the minds of Terence and St John all the morning as a half-comprehended refrain.

> They wrestled up, they wrestled down,
>   They wrestled sore and still:
> The fiend who blinds the eyes of men,
>   That night he had his will.
>
> Like stags full spent, among the bent
>   They dropped awhile to rest—

'Oh, it's intolerable!' Hirst exclaimed, and then checked himself, as if it were a breach of their agreement. (408)

Terence and St John are disturbed not only by the subject of the poem (which they only 'half-comprehend') but also by its repetitive ballad metre — it is the 'sound' of Kingsley's text and the 'beat' of Ridley's walk that distress them. The regular 'beat' of his 'pacing' recalls the marching of Gibbon's prose and that of the armies in 'Street Music' — another indication that this is a rhythmic model antithetical to the 'break[ing]' and 'tumbl[ing]' rhythms of modern writing.[34] Later the same day, a similar experience occurs when Ridley quotes Milton's 'Nativity Ode' (1645). Like all the poems discussed so far, this is a poetic genre that is associated with or aspires to be sung as or represent music. The novel, in other words, quotes numerous texts that imitate or accompany music, and is especially attentive to the rhythmic qualities and effects of these 'hybrid' texts: throughout the novel Ridley is translating Pindar's Odes, and in addition Woolf alludes to the poet-musician Sophocles and quotes part of the libretto of Wagner's *Tristan* and Ariel's song from *The Tempest*. Following her quotations from ballads, songs and 'lays' (in which Macaulay spoke 'in the persons of ancient minstrels'),[35] Woolf quotes the 'hymn' from Milton's 'Ode':

Ridley paced up and down the terrace repeating stanzas of a long poem, in a subdued but suddenly sonorous voice. Fragments of the poem were wafted in at the open window as he passed and repassed.

> Peor and Baalim
> Forsake their Temples dim,
>   With that twice batter'd God of Palestine
> And mooned Astaroth [*sic*] —

The sound of these words were [*sic*] strangely discomforting to both the young men, but they had to be borne. (409)

Not only is Woolf quoting a poetic genre associated with music and one imitative of ancient sung odes, but music is also an important subject of the 'hymn' in the stanzas preceding that which Ridley is reciting. The poet invites the 'heavenly Muse' to 'join thy voice unto the angel choir', and then evokes the celestial 'music sweet' of the nativity and of creation.[36] The delayed cadences of Milton's angelic music suggest that celestial rhythm is sweetly un-emphatic,[37] but the metre of this section of the ode itself (stanza XXII) is more marked. Again, it is its 'sound' rather than the subject matter that disturbs the listening men, though as the subject is the 'drear and dying sound' that accompanies the destruction of the old household deities this might also give them pause for thought.[38] Ridley himself appears almost to be trapped in the rhythm of Milton's poem: the poem's narrative trajectory has been interrupted as he 'repeat[s] stanzas', his oscillation between a soft and 'sonorous' voice mimicking the ode's dramatic contrasts of stasis and turbulence, silence and song. In this, as in so many other passages, the narrator, like the characters, is arguably more interested in the rhythmic and aural qualities than the 'meaning' of poetry. Every example of poetry associated with extreme and painful experiences is a 'musical' genre — one that aspires to evoke or would be accompanied by music. 'Street Music' may have invited the modern writer of poetry and prose to return to 'ancient' metres and to musical rhythms, but the examples quoted in *The Voyage Out* seem instead to represent 'degenerate' 'allegiance[s]' of musical and literary rhythm. These songs, odes and ballads are the antithesis of the varied, individualized rhythms that Woolf associates with modern writing; furthermore, in these quotations, music has a formal, rather than a metaphorical, function and one tied to particular literary genres and conventions. For the twentieth-century writer who must 'invent' as well as 'remember' rhythm, Gibbon's prose and the metric traditions of English poetry are problematic, if enticing, models, represented as repetitive and deathly.[39]

The soporific or disturbing effects of poetic metre and prose rhythm are also attributed to public rhetoric and rhythmic speech in the novel.[40] Spoken and literary rhythms are thus associated with atypical, often extreme, emotional states — illness, distress, grief, day dreaming, and falling in love;[41] it is at these moments that Woolf's characters are most sensitive to rhythm, and rhythm creates or exacerbates these states. Thus, rhythm is repeatedly figured as being not only between media, but also between 'types of experience'.[42] In contrast to the allusions to literary rhythm, however, the novel represents musical rhythm in much more benign terms. There are several references to the music that Rachel is playing or studying (Bach fugues, late Beethoven sonatas, unspecified 'early music' and Wagner's *Tristan und Isolde*), but the longest passage about music concerns the dance at the centre of the novel. This is, furthermore, the only point at which the narrator comments on musical rhythm. The inviting, inclusive effects of the waltz are repeatedly emphasised: the 'old Spaniard' 'fiddled so as to make a tortoise waltz' (167); 'first one couple, then another' join 'the triumphant swing of the waltz' until the 'rhythmic swish of the dancers sounded like a swirling pool' (169); and Rachel and Terence find 'the swing of the dancers and the lilt of the music' 'irresistible' (175). The scene is one of integration and sensuality, a rare moment in which the distinct social groups at the hotel mingle and in which the previously isolated, even solipsistic, Rachel takes a prominent part, first as a dancer then a player. When Rachel takes over from the professional trio, her rhythmic sense allows her to create an innovative performance combining art music, anonymous folk songs and dances:

As very soon she had played the only pieces of dance music she could remember, she went on to play an air from a sonata by Mozart.

'But that's not a dance,' said someone pausing by the piano.

'It is,' she replied, emphatically nodding her head. 'Invent the steps.' Sure of her melody she marked the rhythm boldly so as to simplify the way. Helen caught the idea; seized Miss Allan by the arm, and whirled round the room (. . .). Once their feet fell in with the rhythm they showed a complete lack of self-consciousness. From Mozart Rachel passed without stopping to old English hunting songs, carols, and hymn tunes, for, as she had observed, any good tune, with a little management, became a tune one could dance to. By degrees every person in the room was tripping and turning in pairs or alone. (. . .)

'Now for the great round dance!' Hewet shouted. Instantly a gigantic circle was formed, the dancers holding hands (. . .). (185–6)

It is striking that in a novel so explicitly concerned with writing and with literary-musical relations, the only unequivocally liberating and benign image of rhythm occurs not in connection with literature or even words but with music. This scene provides an alternative rhythmic model to the predominantly male literary canon in the novel and it is one that depicts new versions of old rhythms: Rachel plays old repertoire in a novel way, unconventionally stressing the rhythm of the Mozart sonata. Musical rhythm is remembered and reinvented, just like the dancers' steps. Unlike the disturbing or ambivalent effects of regular poetic metre and Gibbon's prose, the new waltz rhythm stimulates the performer and audience's inventiveness, producing a sense of equitable community.[43] Rachel draws on but 'manage[s]', or reinvents, the canon. The scene emphasizes idiosyncrasy and improvisation; it anticipates, that is, Peter Dayan's observation that 'belief in art' relies on belief in 'individuality, that constant difference' that necessarily 'escapes analysis'.[44] In this scene, fresh rhythm seems to signify creativity or art itself, as it does in Woolf's letters with which we began. The scene literalizes the vision of 'danc[ing]' and 'circl[ing]', 'invent[ing]' and 'remember[ing]' envisaged in 'Street Music'; we might read it, therefore, as a fictional realization of the argument of the essay — as a displaced image of the beneficial effects for artist and aesthetes of experimental, musically-inspired literary rhythm, where music is synonymous with the new and with that which escapes analysis.

Clearly, there is a strong case for reading Woolf's choice of authors and texts in *The Voyage Out* as part of a critique of a patriarchal canon and the privileged masculine education system that undoubtedly disadvantages Rachel. Woolf's careful non-gendering of rhythm in 'Street Music' modulates into a more explicit exploration of gendered literary rhythms in the novel, anticipating her statement in *A Room of One's Own* that '[t]he weight, the pace, the stride of a man's mind are too unlike [a woman writer's] for her to lift anything substantial from him successfully.'[45] Woolf's attention to the gendering of rhythm is only part of the story, however. The novel and 'Street Music' also illustrate rhythm's force as a metaphor for writing or creativity itself, a force recalled in Woolf's later letters. All these texts assert the centrality of rhythm to the composition and appreciation of literature. Woolf's first novel draws on 'Street Music''s vision of regular metre as a socially controlling force, but it has become more negative, its effects distressing and de-humanizing. Both texts represent the dual force of rhythm, which is both liberating and oppressive, and in *The Voyage Out* this duality has become more polarised. Rhythm may be suspect in its anti-individualism — it regiments, it makes people fall in line, whether of dance or battle, it forces its listeners into 'obedience' — but it also represents the very force of art. As 'Street Music' and *The Voyage Out* uneasily acknowledge, this force works by subjecting us to its rhythm, whether the rhythm of Milton's verse, street musicians, or Rachel's piano playing. Whether we feel that as an enchantment and an elevation or as an ensnarement and an alienation depends on our own highly individualised conditions and experience — on gender, sexuality and education, for example. *The Voyage Out* also makes the difficulty — Woolf's own difficulty — of imagining and defining a contemporary rhythmic model of writing an implicit subject of the text itself. As she would later famously write to Smyth: 'though the rhythmical is more natural to me than the narrative, it is completely opposed to the tradition of fiction and I am casting about all the time for some rope to throw the reader'.[46] Woolf's conceptions of positive literary rhythm suggest that it necessarily falls outside critical discourse and canonical conventions in a way that the regular metre of Kingsley, for example, does not. Rather than explicitly articulating a single theory of rhythm, Woolf's ambivalent images 'set [rhythm] working' as a process. Ideal, literary rhythm is thus, for Woolf, literally 'ecstatic' — always outside or beyond what can be rationally and critically known.

NOTES

1 I would like to thank my co-contributors, especially Peter Dayan and David Evans, for their stimulating comments on this essay; their ideas have been invaluable.

2 *The Letters of Virginia Woolf*, edited by Nigel Nicolson and Joanne Trautmann, 6 vols (New York: Harcourt Brace Jovanovich, 1975–80), III, 247 and IV, 303. Hereafter *Letters*.

3 This reflects, of course, the particularly problematic application of this term to prose writing, where it may refer to local details of syntax ('style') or larger organising structures of extended narratives. Tellingly, a recent student handbook of literary terms defines rhythm only as a property of poetry and Angela Leighton recently observed, '[r]hythm is not a literary critical word' — although, as she elegantly demonstrates, its critical imprecision is precisely the point. See X. J. Kennedy, Dana Gioia and Mark Bauerlein, *Handbook of Literary Terms: Literature, Language, Theory*, 2nd edition (n.p., Pearson, 2009) and 'Pater's Music', *The Journal of Pre-Raphaelite Studies* 14 : 2 (Fall, 2005), 67–79 (72). There was, nonetheless, considerable contemporary interest in this topic, from Abram Lipsky's *Rhythm as a Distinguishing Characteristic of Prose Style* (1907), George Saintsbury's *A History of English Prose Rhythm* (1912), and Albert C. Clark's *Prose Rhythm in English* (1913) to, famously, E. M. Forster's *Aspects of the Novel* (1927). The journal *Rhythm* was published in London between 1911 and 1913. Woolf often uses the term with reference to style, although a statement such as 'I am writing [*The Waves*] to a rhythm and not to a plot' (*Letters*, IV, 204) may suggest, as Kate Flint implies, that rhythm also plays a part in the structure of the novel (Virginia Woolf, *The Waves*, edited by Kate Flint (London: Penguin, 1992/2000), xxii).

4 *Letters*, IV, 303.

5 Woolf uses many images of the writer as a rider, for example: 'it was [the woman writer's] trial to take her fence without looking to right or to left.' ('A Room of One's Own', in *A Room of One's Own/Three Guineas*, edited by Michèle Barrett (London, Penguin, 1993), 85.) Given that the letter was written during the typescript revisions of *The Waves*, however, it is possible that there is also a submerged allusion to waves ('white horses') here.

6 *The Diary of Virginia Woolf*, edited by Anne Olivier Bell and Andrew McNeillie, 5 vols (Harmondsworth: Penguin, 1979–1985), V, 339.

7 I do not intend to reassert conventional genre hierarchies here; rather, rhythm plays a part in Woolf's redefinition of 'the literary'. See, for example,

'Letter to a Young Poet' (1932), in which Woolf describes rhythm as 'the most profound and primitive of instincts (of the poet)' and recommends that the modern poet attend to everyday urban rhythms: 'All you need now is to stand at the window and let your rhythmical sense open and shut, open, and shut, boldly and freely, until one thing melts in another, until the taxis are dancing with the daffodils, until a whole has been made from all these separate fragments' (*The Essays of Virginia Woolf: Volume V: 1929–1932*, edited by Stuart N. Clarke (London: Hogarth, 2009), 306–23 (315)).

8   Woolf evokes but inverts the classical association of Pegasus with poetic vision, which may implicitly position the poet as the rider mastering literary conventions in the act of composition. See, for example, Keats's account of 'the high / Imagination' on 'her steeds', and his attack, following Hazlitt, on Johnson and Pope's heroic couplets: 'They sway'd about upon a rocking horse, / And thought it Pegasus' ('Sleep and Poetry', in *Keats's Poetry and Prose*, edited by Jeffrey N. Cox (New York and London: W.W. Norton, 2009), 62–3).

9   See for example Hermione Lee, *Virginia Woolf* (London: Vintage, 1997), 433–4.

10 See for example Sue Roe, *Writing and Gender: Virginia Woolf's Writing Practice* (Hemel Hempstead: Harvester Wheatsheaf, and New York: St. Martin's, 1990), especially 22–3; Woolf, *The Waves*, edited by Kate Flint (London: Penguin, 1992/2000), xxi–xxii, and Angela Smith, *Katherine Mansfield and Virginia Woolf: A Public of Two* (Oxford: Clarendon, 1999), 188–93. Garrett Stewart's dazzling chapter in *Reading Voices: Literature and the Phonotext* (Berkeley and Los Angeles: University of California Press, 1990) analyses the 'slowed phonic pulse' of *The Wave*'s 'permissive' prose that 'lets in as lingual disruption the stray reverberations ordinarily contained or suppressed by the marshaled [*sic*] effects of literary style' (261).

11 See for example 'Music', *Virginia Woolf and the Arts: Selected Papers from the Sixth Annual Conference on Virginia Woolf*, edited by Diane F. Gillespie and Leslie K. Hankins (New York: Pace University Press, 1997), 158–74; Melba Cuddy-Keane, 'Virginia Woolf, Sound Technologies, and the New Aurality', in *Virginia Woolf in the Age of Mechanical Reproduction*, edited by Pamela L. Caughie (New York: Garland, 2000), 69–96; Rishona Zimring, 'Suggestions of Other Worlds: The Art of Sound in *The Years*', *Woolf Studies Annual* 8 (2002), 125–56; Elicia Clements, 'A Different Hearing: Voicing *Night and Day*', *Virginia Woolf Bulletin* 11 (September 2002), 32–9; Elicia Clements, 'Transforming Musical Sounds into Words: Narrative Method in Virginia Woolf's *The Waves*', *Narrative* 13 : 2 (May 2005), 160–81; Angela Frattarola, 'Listening for "Found Sound" Samples in the Novels of Virginia Woolf', *Woolf Studies Annual* 11 (2005), 133–59; and Elicia Clements, 'Virginia Woolf, Ethel Smyth, and Music: Listening as a Productive Mode of Social Interation', *College Literature* 32 : 3 (Summer 2005), 51–71.

12 'Winged Phrases' (1919) refers to Mallarmé in a discussion of George Moore, and 'On Being Ill' (1926) alludes in passing to Mallarmé and Rimbaud. See Elizabeth Steele, *Virginia Woolf's Literary Sources and Allusions: A Guide to the Essays* (New York and London: Garland, 1983), 269 and 196. See also *Letters*, II, 565 and V, 387, 432, 437, and 452.

13 'I think the translations are extremely interesting — also very difficult. The difficulty may be partly that I've left my Mallarmé in London, and thus can't compare them with the French. But I've no doubt at all that they're very good, and give one the same strange feeling as he does. We are inclined to think notes essential, and also that a few pages by you on Mallarmé would make all the difference, and be of the greatest interest' (*Letters*, II, 439).

14 *Letters*, VI, 84. She continued: 'its [*sic*] a fascinating book — and Roger's case about Mallarmé seems to me proved. I shall read it carefully; now I've only dipped.' Woolf owned a copy of Fry's translation and Mallarmé, *Poésies*, 4th edition (Paris: Nouvelle revue française, 1913) (*The Library of Leonard and Virginia Woolf: A Short-title Catalogue*, edited by Julia King and Laila Miletic-Vejzovic, introduction by Diane F. Gillespie (Pullman, WA: Washington State University Press, 2003), 145). In her biography of Fry (1940), Woolf writes of Fry sharing the 'dangerous delight' of translation with his visitors, and notes his/their attention to the sound of Mallarmé's poems: 'if it was impossible to find the exact sense, let alone the exact sound, Mallarmé, intoned in Roger Fry's deep and resonant voice, filled the dining-room with magnificent reverberations' (Virginia Woolf, *Roger Fry: A Biography* (London: Vintage, 2003), 239. See also 288).

15 Louise A. DeSalvo, *Virginia Woolf's First Voyage: A Novel in the Making* (London: Macmillan, 1980), 3. DeSalvo proposes composition had begun by early 1908.

16 *The Voyage Out*, edited by Lorna Sage (Oxford: Oxford University Press, 1992), 4–6. Henceforth cited parenthetically.

17 This device recurs: the opening passage about the Ambroses is echoed at the end of the novel when Mrs Flushing weeps over Rachel's death, un-consoled by her husband (418).

18 *The Essays of Virginia Woolf: Volume I: 1904–1912*, edited by Andrew McNeillie (London: Hogarth, 1986/1995), 27–32. Henceforth cited parenthetically.

19 One significant exception is Anna Snaith's plenary lecture, '*The Years*, Street Music and Acoustic Space', at the International Virginia Woolf conference, Fordham University, New York, June 2009. I am very grateful to Anna Snaith for her generosity in sharing this work and for her helpful comments on this essay.

20 *A Room of One's Own*, 87.

21 *Letters*, I, 190 and 180.

22 See Garrett Stewart, who describes 'phonic' language, following Kristeva, as 'not necessarily a gendered phenomenon', but instead 'a polymorphous eroticism of the voice' (*Reading Voices*, 278).

23 See also Woolf's 1903 diary account 'A Dance in Queens Gate', in Virginia Woolf, *A Passionate Apprentice: The Early Journals 1897–1909*, edited by Mitchell A. Leaska (San Diego, CA, Harvest and New York: Harcourt Brace Jovanovich, 1992), 164–7.

24 *Letters*, I, 88.

25 Snaith, however, persuasively places the essay in the context of xenophobic and snobbish English attacks on street musicians; if the essay is read as a direct response to hostile contemporary discourses about street musicians, the tone — and Woolf's championing of 'the poor' — appear less ironic.

26 See Brad Bucknell, *Literary Modernism and Musical Aesthetics: Pater, Pound, Joyce, and Stein* (Cambridge: Cambridge University Press, 2001).

27 The *OED* attributes the first use of this term to 'On Ancient Greek Rhythm and Metre' (1864), in *Essays Philological and Critical Collected from the Papers of James Hadley* (London: Macmillan, 1873), 95.

28 See 'On Not Knowing Greek' (1925), *The Essays of Virginia Woolf: Volume IV: 1925–1928*, edited by Andrew McNeillie (London: Hogarth, 1994/2002), 38–53. The opening sentence states 'we do not know how the words sounded' (38); see also 43 and 48. There is an important argument to be made about Woolf's more precise conceptions and use of Apolline and Dionysian rhythms in 'Street Music' and *The Voyage Out*, though this lies outside my attention to Woolf's metaphorical deployment of rhythm. I am very grateful to Jim Stewart for sharing his work on this subject with me.

29 Cf. Peter Dayan's account of unheard yet 'remembered' music in Proust, in *Music Writing Literature, from Sand via Debussy to Derrida* (Aldershot: Ashgate, 2006), 80–2.

30 *A Room of One's Own*, 69. Furthermore, 'the glory which [Rachel] had perceived at first [in Gibbon] had faded, and, read as she would, she could not grasp the rhythm' (226).

31 Cf. Pater's statement in 'The School of Giorgione', that 'true poetical quality' 'comes of an inventive handling of rhythmical language', cited in Leighton, 73, and Vernon Lee's adoption of the term in *The Handling of Words and Other Studies in Literary Psychology* (1923). For Pater's influence on Woolf (though with no discussion of rhythm), see Perry Meisel, *The Absent Father: Virginia Woolf and Walter Pater* (New Haven and London: Yale University Press, 1980), and for a suggestive analysis of Pater's rhythmic prose see Leighton.

32 'A Masque', l. 853, in John Milton, *Odes, Pastorals, Masques*, edited by J. B. Broadbent (Cambridge: Cambridge University Press, 1975), 152. Woolf read the parts of the Lady and Sabrina in an amateur performance of the masque around early 1908. See Lee, 252.

33   See Milton, 152, note.

34   See Helen Abbott's observations elsewhere in this volume on regular rhythm and walking.

35   Lord Macaulay, *'Lays of Ancient Rome' with 'Ivry' and 'The Armada'* (London: Longmans, Green and Co., 1883), 24.

36   John Milton, 'On the Morning of Christ's Nativity', ll. 15, 27 and 93 (*Odes, Pastorals, Masques*, 15, 16 and 19).

37   'The air . . . / With thousand echoes still prolongs each heavenly close', 'On the Morning of Christ's Nativity', ll. 99–100 (19).

38   'On the Morning of Christ's Nativity', l. 193 (24).

39   Sue Roe proposes that, in *To the Lighthouse* (1927), Woolf represents poetic metre as an 'illusion', 'a structure for experience which comes fully formed' (Roe, 69). The repeated images of Mr Ramsay's pacing and declamation also, famously, recall Woolf's father Leslie Stephen. Similarly, St John's play is implicitly characterised as mechanical or schematic when Rachel admires the 'skill of his rhythms and the variety of his adjectives' (260), and his lack of rhythmic sensibility is underscored at the dance when Rachel's 'good ear for rhythm' is 'incompatible' with his 'anatomy of a waltz' (170).

40   Helen echoes St John's words, for example, 'rhythmically and absent-mindedly' (230), while Susan Warrington's 'voice proceeded rhythmically as if checking the list' when she lists her domestic obligations and activities, 'in a mild ecstasy of satisfaction with her life and her own nature' (304). Rachel's abrupt rejection of Christianity, which follows her perception that the 'swing' of rhetoric prevents her from 'listen[ing] critically', is prompted by her sensitivity to musical rhythm: 'Such was the discomfort she felt when forced to sit through an unsatisfactory piece of music badly played. Tantalized, enraged by the clumsy insensitiveness of the conductor, who put the stress on the wrong places, and annoyed by the vast flock of the audience tamely praising and acquiescing without knowing or caring, so she was now tantalized and enraged' (264).

41   See for example 210–11, where Terence shouts 'nonsense' about Rachel.

42   See the Introduction to this volume, [150].

43   Compare the repetitive rhythm of the waltz in *The Years*: 'The waltz music took the words "calling and answering each other" and flung them out; but as it repeated the same rhythm again and again, it coarsened them, it destroyed them. The dance music interfered with everything. At first exciting, then it became boring and finally intolerable' (*The Years*, edited by Hermione Lee, with notes by Sue Asbee (Oxford: Oxford University Press, 1992/2000), 129).

44   Dayan, 73.

45   *A Room of One's Own*, 69.

46   *Letters*, IV, 204.

Boomboom and Hullabaloo: Rhythm in the Zurich Dada Revolution

David Gascoigne

Abstract:

The drumbeats which punctuated Zurich Dada performances signal and enact the dismantling of the complexities of a culture the participants deemed wholly discredited. While the Futurists looked to technology for rhythmic renewal, Dadaists sought a deeper, more indefinable rhythm to nourish a far-reaching renaissance of human values. Study of 'nonsensical' texts by Huelsenbeck, Ball and Tzara reveals some traditional metrical elements. However, in Dadaist performance pieces in an imaginary hybrid language or in a 'simultaneous poem' in three languages at once, such elements are freed from traditional associations and become multiple, complex and ambiguous in performance and reception.

Keywords: rhythm, Dada, drumbeat, Futurism, metrics, nonsense poem, simultaneous poem, multilingualism

Tristan Tzara, writing in his Dada Manifesto of 1918, expressed with characteristic verve the Dadaists' celebration of the collapse of contemporary culture:

Behold a tottering world in flight, wedded to the tinkling bells playing the scales of hell, behold on the other side: new men. Rough, bounding, bestriders of hiccups. (...) We (...) are preparing the great spectacle of disaster, fire, decomposition. Are preparing the suppression of mourning and replacing tears by sirens stretched from one continent to another.[1]

A striking feature of this virtuoso invective is the way the antagonists are characterized by sounds associated with them. The tottering culture in decay is wedded to the tinkle of its fool's bells, at once ridiculous and hellish, while the Dadaists, as horsemen ushering in the apocalypse to the worldwide wail of sirens, leap forward propelled by the staccato sound of ... hiccups. Or perhaps the word 'hoquets' here suggests spasms of fear, or death-throes, or the cough of a faltering machine? Any of these connotations can convey the same Ubuesque

Paragraph 33:2 (2010) 197–214
DOI: 10.3366/E0264833410000842

compound of the farcical and the sinister as is epitomized by the hellish fool's bells ('grelots').[2] What is clear is that a battle between old and new is to be conducted through the medium of noise. Tzara goes on to target specifically the intelligentsia's reception of literary work:

If I cry:

> *Ideal, ideal, ideal*
> *Knowledge, knowledge, knowledge,*
> *Boomboom, boomboom, boomboom*

I have recorded pretty precisely the progress, law, morality and all the other fine qualities which various very intelligent people have discussed in so many books, only to end up, finally, saying that, in any case, everyone has danced in time to his own personal boomboom, and that he's quite right in his boomboom. (*OC* I, 363)

Again, the irreducible individuality of authentic writing as Tzara sees it is conveyed through the attribute which transcends all moralising and idealising commentaries, and which is that essential 'boomboom' which energises it. The insistent repetition we find here of the word 'boomboom' is wholly unsurprising in this Dada manifesto, given the role which explosive drumbeats had played in the Zurich Dada cabaret evenings in which Tzara had collaborated the previous year. 'Boomboom' had emerged as the rhythmic call-sign of the Dada enterprise. The term itself, however, does not provide any suggestion as to what kind of significance is to be attached to this beat, and the reiteration of the simple onomatopoeic word carries Tzara's mockery and defiance of the intellectualization he is here dismissing.

In the highly eclectic 'Cabaret Voltaire' evenings during which the Dadaists presented their work, deafening thumps on the bass drum accompanied Richard Huelsenbeck's recitations of poetry penned by himself or others; he would beat time to the text, frequently delivered in a fortissimo shout, and delighted in disturbing and provoking the audience to fury and indignation. His description conveys his enthusiasm: 'It was a witches' sabbath, (. . .) a hullabaloo from morning to night, a frenzy of drums and negro tom-toms. (. . .) Together we made a magnificent negro song with rattles, wooden clappers and lots of primitive instruments.'[3] This performance poetry required, it seems, a percussive soundtrack to envelop it, and drums to energize it. But was this primitive and improvised music intended to reinforce the heard rhythms of the text, or to challenge that verbal utterance with the stuff of non-verbal rhythm? In the collective effort to generate an art (or anti-art) of protest and renewal, the drumbeat could fulfil many functions. It was powerful enough to attract attention in any circumstances, and to cut through the ambient noise of a conservative or hostile audience, thus representing the potency of the lone dissident voice operating within a culture of apathy or reactionary consensus. Further, it evoked the down-market art of street-performers and popular cabaret, which reflected the Dadaists' debunking of traditional high culture. It could parody the bombastic militarism of the warring regimes, or indeed the actual pounding of the cannon in the trenches, which many of the performers had fled to Zurich to escape. Moreover, the references Huelsenbeck makes here to performances of so-called 'negro poetry' point up how this sub-genre of Dadaist practice offered special opportunities for a combination of chanting and drumming. Some of these 'negro' pieces were genuine transcriptions of ethnic oral poetry culled by Tzara from published anthologies and anthropological journals, while others, including most of Huelsenbeck's contributions in this category, were semi-improvised nonsense texts in imitation of non-European languages. Given that few if any in the audience would have been able to recognize whether a text of this kind was authentic, let alone understand it if it were, the public performance of such pieces clearly functioned on one level as a frontal assault on the conventions of poetry performance as communication with an audience. On another level, however, it signified for the Dadaists a means of suggesting an alternative untainted source of vitality to replace the hopelessly compromised European canon, one of the new points of departure to be exploited by Tzara's 'new, rough, bounding men'. Over and above all these associations (military, vaudeville, ethnic), the beat of a drum possessed an abstract, talismanic quality: as a manifestation of rhythm it is both irreducibly elemental and indefinitely polysemic in its significance, provisionally structuring through its pulses of energy the passage of time, but *expressing* nothing definable. As such, the drumbeat, as a potent yet open-ended challenge, had enormous appeal to the Dadaists, devoted as they all were (whatever their individual differences) to the notion of sweeping away a corrupt culture and founding a new environment for creative exploration based on a rediscovery of the most elemental constituents of art and expression. The insistent 'boomboom' of the drum represented a dismantling of complexity and of meaning, which was the necessary first step in the purging of a rotten culture.

In his text for voices 'La première aventure céleste de M. Antipyrine'[4] which was performed and published in July 1916, Tzara names one of the voices 'Mr. Boumboum'. Henri Béhar suggests in his notes to this text that it evokes a Dada circus, whose ringmaster, Mr Boumboum, takes it upon himself to make as much noise as possible, and that the circus-ring can be seen as a metaphor for war-torn Europe. Given that the text attempts a kind of multiple-voice performance poetry, Béhar's reading could be extended to suggest that the performance-text-as-circus exemplifies Dadaist poetry in action, and that, as Tzara conveyed in his 1918 manifesto, the rhythmic 'boomboom' is indeed the ringmaster in the cabaret-act of this whole enterprise.

The Dadaists gleaned ideas and performance techniques from other European avant-garde movements such as Marinetti and the Futurists, and shared with them the conviction that the European crisis was the benighted product of an entire history of progressively degraded culture and ideology. They surpassed the Futurists, however, in their comprehensive hostility to the status quo, as can be illustrated in at least two important respects, relating to technology and to nationalism. The Futurists were passionately enthusiastic about modern technology, singing the praises of electricity, of trams and fast motor-cars, and savouring the vocabulary associated with these innovations. Technology exemplified — was seen even as indispensable to — the new dynamism they wished to inject into culture. The Dadaists, on the other hand, were in general deeply suspicious of this technological revolution, and viewed current military-industrial machine-culture rather as destructive of human beings and human values. This disagreement affects their attitudes to rhythm. The Futurists declared that machines, by imposing their rapid rhythm charged with the acceleration of modern life, suggested a way for art to become more material, rapid and direct, with simplified syntax, abbreviation and onomatopoeia.[5] Where the Dadaists exploited such noises and rhythms, however, the effect was never to illustrate their prestige but rather to attack and subvert it.

Secondly, the Futurists, and their Parisian admirers, were highly patriotic in their view of the war. Pierre-Albert Birot, for instance, urged his French readership to heed the example of the Germans' nationalist ambitions, and argued that the patriotism enshrined in the slogan 'Deutschland über alles' should characterize any nation worth the name.[6] Such a stance is at the opposite pole from the ideas and actions of the exiled draft-dodgers, individualists and revolutionaries who made up the Zurich Dada group. As for the Italian futurists, their nationalistic and military fervour was even more emphatic: their pamphlet 'Sintesi futurista della guerra' (Futurist Synthesis of the War) glorified war as a necessary 'purging' of the world, but declared that this mission of destroying the past could only be entrusted to the virile youth and creative genius of Italy, rather than 'medieval, plagiarist, clumsy Germany'.[7] Thus the Futurists linked the liberation of artistic expression to the renewal of nationhood, in a proto-fascist spirit. For the Dadaists, the war carried no purgative virtue, and such nationalist flag-waving was a manifestation of the disease, not the cure.

While the Dada group was agreed on the urgent need to dismantle a civilization marked by mechanization, consumerism and the debased currency of patriotic and moralizing slogans, they shared no common view as to where any new starting-point might be found for a future renaissance of the spirit. Tzara's distinctly cynical and nihilist turn of mind contrasted sharply with Ball's metaphysical idealism and Arp's aspiration to a purity of aesthetic abstraction. Yet such tentative conceptions of renewal as they touched on often evoke the notion of rhythm as something fundamental to it. For Marinetti and Birot, the matter was simpler: it was the energizing rhythm of modern technology which could provide an inspiration and a model for art. Such Dadaist pronouncements as one can find are however both more allusive and more profound. In April 1916 Ball tries to sum up what underlies the group's highly diverse initiatives: 'Our debates are a burning search, more blatant every day, for the specific rhythm, for the buried face of this age — for its basis and its essence; for the possibility of its being seized and woken. Art is only an opportunity for that, a method.'[8] The Dada cabaret here emerges as a laboratory whose central project, through a wide variety of artistic experiments, is to locate a deep rhythm which is vitally central to culture, and which needs to be grasped and reactivated. As a strategy for these experiments: 'Adopt symmetries and rhythms instead of principles. Confute world orders and acts of state by transforming them into a phrase or a brush-stroke.'[9] Art is thus a method for taking the corrupt political and cultural order of the world, and draining it of 'principle', of ideological content by incorporating it into a symmetry or a rhythm which is wholly independent of it — an alchemy of subversion. Tzara for his part writes of two different kinds of rhythm: one audible and banal, 'the beating of a shrivelled heart, fool's bells of putrid spongey wood', the other inward and ungraspable, wherein lies perhaps the key to a new order: 'Rhythm is the trotting of intonations you can hear; there is a rhythm which you cannot see or hear, light-rays from an inner cluster towards a constellation of order.'[10] As our opening quotation showed, the 'fool's bells' are the derisory music of contemporary decay. In response, rhythm in poetry is, on the surface, present in the metrical patterns perceived by the listener — but there is a more foundational if unidentifiable rhythm, which can radiate out from an individual utterance towards a new order of significance. This inner rhythm which can be sensed even if not precisely located in authentic poetry constitutes what Tzara termed the 'personal boomboom'. Despite their very different temperaments and attitudes, Tzara and Ball share this vision of a rhythm which is mysterious and buried deep, but which needs to be touched on and awoken if the alchemy of renaissance is to be worked.

For audiences at the Cabaret Voltaire, however, such metaphysical or even mystical considerations must have seemed a world away. Confronted as they were with spoken texts which at best flouted the norms of communication and at worst were couched in a wholly alien or nonsense language, for them the drumbeat may at times have seemed like the only organizing principle. This priority given to rhythm, at the expense of coherent meaning, recognizable literary structure or the musicality of poetic language, becomes a dominant feature in some areas of Dadaist experimental writing. The drumbeat effect can be crudely obvious, as in the insistent trochaic rhythm of 'Capriccio', a poem by Huelsenbeck from 1916, which begins:

Jammer brüllen. Affen heulen.	(Wailings yelling. Monkeys howling.
Gluten klammen	Embers clamming
Klammen Klauben	clamming culling
Bimmel Baumel	jangle dangle
Bummel Bummel	dawdle dawdle
in die Nacht.[11]	into night.)[12]

The evocation of darkness and horror, recurrent in a good deal of this writing, operates here through a degradation of articulate language into near-meaningless chant in the space of five lines, even though overall syntactic structure is more or less respected. The words in lines 3–5 are, in themselves, meaningful or potentially meaningful, but are evidently primarily aligned for alliterative and rhythmic effect. Another aspect of the effect of rhythm is shown in 'Die Primitiven'

(The Primitives), a poem Huelsenbeck included in his extended work *Phantastische Gebete* (Fantastic Prayers), sections of which figured frequently in the Cabaret Voltaire programmes. Its opening lines read as follows:

indigo, indigo	(indigo, indigo
Trambahn, Schlafsack	tramway, sleeping-bag
Wanz und Floh	bedbug and flea
indigo indigai	indigo, indigai
umbaliska	umbaliska
bumm Dadai.[13]	boom Dadai.)

Here the tone is more playful, with the text oscillating between nonsense language and a seemingly inconsequential sequence of real words which, if they constitute meaning at all, do no more than evoke the marginal life-style of the Dada group (tramway, sleeping-bag, bedbug, flea). The excerpt ends with the typically self-advertising beat ('bumm Dadai') of the Dada drum.

Reading this piece aloud reveals, firstly, the alternation of dactyls and trochees within a regular beat, and, secondly, a symmetry in both rhyme (ABA, CDC) and rhythm between lines 1–3 and lines 4–6, signalled by the near-repeat of the 'indigo' line. The analogies all this suggests are with the steady pulse of children's skipping rhymes, or (for Anglophone readers) with the verse of Edward Lear, which similarly mixes standard and nonsense words. The equivalent associations for German readers would have included the witty light verse, popular with both children and adults at this period, of Christian Morgenstern. The similarities in tone and technique with childhood verse are not fortuitous: the language and sensibility of children, like that of 'negroes', represented another possible point of new departure for Dada, in the work of deconstructing civilization. The very word 'Dada', one of the first sounds a child may pronounce in many cultures, suggests this point of reference. The echoes of nursery or playground rhyming, reinforced by predictable rhyming patterns, foreground the importance of rhythms in the reader's construction of meaning in the text.

Ball, however, produced some more radically experimental texts written for performance in the cabaret in which the role of rhythm becomes more startlingly dynamic, given the weakening of the other conventional parameters of sense or structure. At least two such poems, in Ball's reading of them, became iconic items in Zurich

Dada's repertoire. One of these, 'Karawane', is a text of seventeen unpunctuated lines of varying length, and begins:

> jolifanto bambla o falli bambla
> grossgiga m'pfa habla horem
> egiga goramen
> higo bloiko russula huju[14]

The opening word 'jolifanto' offers one handhold to the bemused listener: its similarity to 'Elefant' seems to be reinforced later on by 'russula' (cf. 'Rüssel' = 'elephant's trunk', in German) and these, together with the title 'Karawane', compose a fragile framework of sense (an elephant caravan), a hypothesis later confirmed by Ball himself.[15] This nevertheless leaves the particular nature of most elements of the text unexplained. No syntactic structure can be safely deduced from the word-sequences, especially since the individual words seem so linguistically diverse in nature.[16] The poem reaches a climax of compression in line 10 which consists of a single repeated vowel, 'ü üü ü'—perhaps the point at which even nonsense language dissolves into noise (elephant-trumpeting?)—before concluding in sound-patterns of incantation and muffled percussion, again suggesting heavy dactylic/trochaic rhythms within a steady tactus:

> wulubu ssubudu uluwu ssubudu
> tumba ba-umf
> kusa gauma
> ba - umf

The final repeated 'ba-umf' echoes the chant of 'umba, umba' with which Huelsenbeck customarily punctuated his performances of 'negro' poetry: the Zurich Dadaists constantly borrowed words, ideas and images from each other, or developed them in collaboration. Here, the 'exotic' subject of elephants may have favoured this drumbeat echo.

Ball's more sustained experimental poem 'Gadji beri bimba', again of seventeen lines, presents a significantly more radical challenge. The opening reads as follows:

> gadji beri bimba glandridi laula lonni cadori
> gadjama gramma berida bimbala glandri galassassa laulitalomini[17]

As in 'Karawane', few of the constituent words offer any immediate meaning, and hence the text provides no semantic coherence. Unlike

'Karawane', there is no title to offer a hint of a frame of reference, although words such as 'rhinozerossola' (ll. 5, 6), 'zanzibar' (8), 'elifantolim' (9), 'negramai' (twice in 13) clearly suggest a similar strain of exoticism. Nevertheless, this still leaves 111 of the 117 words of the poem to grapple with.

The reader is in fact left with little option but to deal with the nonsense-language in its own terms, that is, in terms of its pseudo-linguistic features and of its likely characteristics as an 'abstract' structure of sound-sequences when presented in oral performance. On this level, there are arguably three principal features which can be seen to lend the text a degree of (non-semantic) cohesion: these are phonic repetition, pseudo-morphology and, most important of all, rhythm.

Firstly, the nature and effect of phonic repetition in this text can be briefly illustrated from line 8, the opening line of the second section:

zimzim urallala zimzim urallala zimzim zanzibar zimzalla zam

The repetition here of 'zimzim urallala' and of the phoneme 'zim' is part of a wide network of reiterations and echoes within the text. 'Zimzalla' (ll. 4, 8) in turn links by assonance to 'bimbala' (2, 14) and thereby to another family-group of words running from 'bimba' (1), to 'bim', 'bin', 'ban' and 'binban' (3, 4), and on to 'bimbalo' (and 'pimpalo') (11), and 'bumbalo' (13, 15). Likewise, the repeated 'urallala' finds antecedents in 'laula' (1) and 'terrullala blaulala' (7) and feeds into a larger clutch of words all ending in '-al(l)a'. Such networks of phonic repetition carry an implication of order rather than disorder: the fact of repetition, at this level of density, suggests to a listener that the choice and sequence of verbal components is not random, but governed by some limiting principle or underlying system, whether the implied order be that of a meaningful linguistic idiom unknown or unavailable to the listener or whether, more likely, it be that of a performative, 'magic' language, akin to shamanic utterance or 'speaking in tongues'. The conjunction of 'zimzalla binban' would have recalled for German speakers a well-known nursery song, dating from the eighteenth century: 'Auf einem Baum ein Kuckuck / simsaladim bamba saladu saladim / Auf einem Baum ein Kuckuck sass' (Upon a tree a cuckoo sat). The nonsense line ('simsaladim...') is repeated in each of the six verses of this song, and seems to have acquired the status of a formulaic magic spell, like 'abracadabra' in English.[18]

A second feature of the text, which I have dubbed pseudo-morphology, is already apparent in the sequence of words which open the first four lines: 'gadji', 'gadjama', 'gadji', 'gadjama'. The pattern thus created implies morphological variation on a common root, and this is reinforced by similarly mutating pairs of words occurring within the first three lines: 'beri'/'berida', 'bimba'/'bimbala', 'glandridi'/'glandri', 'laula'/'laulitalomini', 'cadori'/'cadorsu'. The word-sequence of the text thus behaves like an inflected language, carrying in this respect also a suggestion of structure and meaning. Nonsense texts work best when they tempt the reader or listener with a possible sense, exploiting the rich border territory between fully meaningful utterance and random noise. Both phonic repetition and pseudomorphology are here exploited to create that tantalized hesitancy in the listener — but what would really grip his/her attention in performance would be the rhythmic pulse of the piece.

The rhythmic pattern of this poem is not a given: it must be inferred. While no stress-patterns are marked in the text, its pseudo-morphological aspect strongly encourages any performer of it to place the stress on the opening syllable of the interrelated bisyllabic or trisyllabic words. This would accord with Ball's likely instinct as a native German speaker to place the stress on the root syllable, as in for example *Líebe*, *líeblich*, *Líebende*. If this is done, what we hear throughout the piece in performance will be a heavily marked sequence of (mostly) trochaic and dactylic rhythms. Where the dactyls predominate, the pace quickens, as in lines 5 and 13 ('ó katalóminai rhínozeróssola. . .', 'túffm im zímbrabim négramai búmbalo. . .'), and arguably becomes positively headlong in the galloping 2 + 4 rhythms of line 8, quoted above ('zímzim úrallala. . .'), with the implicit drumbeat tactus being further subdivided.

In the final stanza of the poem, however, the closing lines reverse the processes of morphological augmentation, phonic enrichment and bursts of acceleration. The series of strong initial words of the first four lines of the poem (gadji, gadjama) is picked up again, but now, in the last four lines, 'gadjama' and 'gadjamen' are ignominiously displaced by 'gaga', occurring in each of these lines, with its overtones (in French and English, at least) of infantilism, madness or senility;

> gadjama bimbala oo beri gadjama gaga di gadjama affalo pinx
> gaga di bumbalo bumbalo gadjamen
> gaga di bling blong
> gaga blung

The rhythmic momentum falters and dies in a jumble of stresses, with the dactylic percussion of 'bumbalo bumbalo' giving way to the increasingly muffled bell sounds of 'bling blong (...) blung', ending the whole piece on a closed nasal vibration.

The sonic effect of the piece is that of a collage of different sound colours combining like instruments in an orchestra, with each developing group of words commencing in 'g' or 'b', 'z' or 'l' contributing its particular sonority. The whole poem is animated in performance by a strong ebb and flow in rhythmic patterns, in implied tempo and in variety of attack from short sharp sounds to prolonged vowels, from hard consonants to liquid '–lo' or '–la' endings.[19] While this text remains a more or less sense-less experiment, functioning at or beyond the limits of the meaningful, it nevertheless demonstrates some success in building a provisional poetic structure out of emphatically non-semantic elements which encourage the reader to turn to rhythm as the guiding principle in the process of constructing conditional meanings.

From the vantage-point of the twenty-first century, Ball's project in this text can be seen as an experiment in deconstruction-reconstruction within language and poetics. He has radically dismantled any appearance of semantic coherence by writing in an unrecognizable personal language which itself suggests a fusion of a whole range of linguistic idioms without privileging any of them. The text he writes is, however, not devoid of implicit structure, as we have seen, but such patterns as there are suggest a liberation of the repertoires of sound and rhythm in their most basic forms from dependence on any preconceived overriding meaning and on any particular cultural context. Within this performance discourse, language is broken down into some of its constituents, and these syllabic, phonic and rhythmic constituents reconfigured in a novel and unpredictable form, shorn as far as possible of the contextual immersion in (or contamination by) the despised prevailing European culture.

The effort of emancipation from any particular national or linguistic culture which Ball attempts here finds even more dramatic expression in some of the collaborative works of the Dadaists. The participants in Zurich Dada each characteristically spoke several languages, and enjoyed contriving multilingual pieces between them — Tzara (Rumanian), Arp (Alsatian) and Walter Serner (German) played at writing poems, each contributing in turn, with alternating lines or couplets in French and German, to produce a kind of modernist macaronic verse. The principles of this private entertainment in multi-lingualism were then extended as the basis for a new performance genre, the 'poème simultan'. One example of this form was entitled 'L'Amiral cherche une maison à louer' (The Admiral seeks a house to rent), and was first performed at the Cabaret Voltaire by Tzara, Huelsenbeck and Marcel Janco on 30 March 1916.[20] Tzara's text was in French, Huelsenbeck's in German and Janco's in English, the three being declaimed simultaneously, according to a layout determined by Tzara ensuring that they would start and finish together, and that at certain points a single voice might momentarily be heard solo. The performers also wielded noise-making devices — a whistle, castanets, and of course a drum for Huelsenbeck — and Tzara's layout stipulates a sudden 'orchestral' interlude in mid-performance for these instruments, with specified rhythms and dynamics, accompanied only by repeated exclamations ('rouge bleu', 'hihi Yabomm').

While Tzara apparently co-ordinated this performance and determined its shape, one can assume that each of the three contributed his own text. Huelsenbeck's text reflects here and there the narrative idea which the title seems to announce, the admiral's quest for a house to rent — but the admiral's trousers fall apart right at the start ('Des Admirals gwirktes Beinkleid schnell zerfällt'). Thereafter, while the text is very discontinuous and punctuated with percussive lines of vocal noise, such as 'chrrza prrrza' or 'pataclan patablan', further details accumulate to evoke some grotesque and sordid carnal encounter. Examples of this are references to the rattlesnake-green ('Klapperschlangengrün') of the concierge's stomachs, the admiral's sweetly swollen evening rendez-vous ('O süss gequollnes Stelldichein'), a notice (is it?) directing inhabitants to the toilet ('Wer Wasser braucht find im Klosett/ zumeistens was er nötig hätt' — 'Anyone requiring water will generally find what they need in the lavatory') and the possible innuendo of the biblical reference in the line 'Wem suchet, dem wird aufgetan' (to him who seeks it shall be opened). The tone at the end becomes more cataclysmic, with the bellowing of animals, fire in Yoshiwara (a red-light district of Tokyo), a whipping round the loins and a high-priest's obscene exposure: 'Im Schlafsack gröhlt der alte Oberpriester/ Und zeigt der Schenkel volle Tastatur' (In his sleeping-bag the old high priest bawls/ and reveals the whole keyboard of his thighs). Whatever brief satisfaction is achieved ('O süss gequollnes Stelldichein') it all ends in brimstone, and the laying bare of obscenity. The poem concludes with the three voices declaiming in unison, in French: 'L'amiral n'a rien trouvé' (The admiral hasn't found anything).

Similarly, throughout the poem, the reader has been challenged to hunt for meaning in the polyrhythmic fabric, but that search must remain fruitless; while rhythm seems to point towards patterns of meaning which slip in and out of focus, it must ultimately lead us nowhere, raising only more questions where we might be tempted to believe it could provide answers.

The French text recited by Tzara seems more whimsical. His opening words 'Boum boum boum/ Il déshabilla sa chair' (he undressed his flesh) perhaps parallels the admiral's lost breeches in Huelsenbeck's text, and a concierge again figures, a deceitful one who has sold the apartment which the speaker had rented. There are other possible echoes: mention of 'l'âme du serpent à Bucarest' (the soul of the snake at Bucharest) occurs close to the word 'Klapperschlangengrün', and the hint of death and an obscene apocalypse recurs here with falling birds and shitting archangels. But the French text is even more discontinuous in tone and substance — the irruption of fragments of conversation ('Et c'est très intéressant' or 'Oh! Mon cher c'est si difficile') is reminiscent of Laforgue, a strong influence on Tzara's early poems. If it is difficult to discover in Tzara's text any coherent thematic or narrative pattern linking the disparate elements of this collage — a concierge's betrayal, what the fisherman said to the countess, images of a train creeping away like a wounded animal, of a lighthouse with its circling birds, or of (what might be) a film called 'je vous adore' on show at the 'sycomore casino' — then this may partly be accounted for by the fact that the poem recycles some elements of Tzara's earlier poetry, originally written in Rumanian.[21]

One aspect of both Huelsenbeck's and Tzara's texts does however become apparent to anyone who reads them aloud, and that is an intermittent reliance on some formal features of verse. Huelsenbeck's text is propelled forward by traditional metrical patterns — after a naval call to attention ('Ahoi ahoi'), the opening lines alternate hexameter and pentameter, with even the line of vocal noise adopting and reinforcing the regular rhythm. The verse then lapses into more popular patter form, as in the lines beginning 'Wer suchet' and 'Wer Wasser braucht' already quoted. This rhythmic beat is reinforced by a number of conventional rhymes. Remarkably, the last word in German, 'Tastatur', rhymes with 'Natur' in line 5, each closing a pentameter line. Tzara's text is also partly structured by rhymes (dorénavant/ éléphants/restaurant, messe/comtesse); midway through there are pairs of weak rhymes in — é (trompé/loué, fumée/écrasés), and the text ends with a concentration of internal rhyme: 'prore' (a nonsense word?), 'adore', 'sycomore'. In general, then, insofar as there are any elements of structure within these two texts, they are to be found more at the level of rhythm, metre and rhyme than at that of sense or imagery. These formal characteristics point towards patterns of meaning, but they are always elusive, conflictual, disturbing. The third text, sung in English, or rather in American, is even more obviously a collage. Janco, one could assume, had no native command of English, and so his contribution is, in two identifiable sections, a patchwork of (ill-spelt) fragments of American popular songs of the period. The opening lines ('Where the honeysuckle vine twines itself round the door/ A sweetheart mine is waiting patiently for me') are taken from a sentimental 1914 song entitled 'Rebecca of Sunnybrook Farm', and later on Janco throws in a snatch from Irving Berlin's well-known hit 'Everybody's Doin' It Now'. The lyrics of these songs fall of course into comparable conventional patter forms as occur occasionally in the other two texts, and so, with the throwing together of these different ingredients — of German grotesque nightmare, French pre-surrealist whimsy and a jumble of frothy American pop-songs — the brew of the simultaneous poem is contrived, in a mixture in which, as often in cuisine, few of the ingredients remain distinct and separately identifiable.

We can conclude from this that the audience's experience here will be less one of verbal communication than of rhythmic stimulus and a kind of strange, quasi-improvised polylingual music. Certainly meaning is sacrificed to sound, both in terms of the spoken texts impeding each other (like picking up three radio stations at once on the same wavelength), and also in terms of the interlude at the centre where extraneous noise and robotic utterance take over from the polylingual counterpoint. One objective of the piece was clearly to disrupt and confuse the audience's reception and focus. Just as each individual text is unstable in meaning and direction, the aggregation of them in performance creates for the listener a collective manifestation of disorientation and incoherence.

The wider strategies which underlie the very radical form of this piece, and the others like it, can usefully be placed in the context of the overall (post-Nietzschean) Dadaist project of destruction and revolutionary reconstruction. Firstly, and in context perhaps most obviously, the poem could be viewed, on the destructive side, as reflecting Dada's anti-war sentiment, in that this aggressive pitching of one language against another can be taken as a parodic metaphor for the war which was raging between the combatant nations.

In this perspective the ending, when all three voices come together for the first time to declare that 'L'Amiral n'a rien trouvé', can be read as a proclamation of the bankruptcy of militaristic and hierarchical society. An alternative and apparently opposite view is to take the polylingualism of this piece as a model of internationalism, of the confluence of different cultures.[22] For the Dadaists, cosmopolitan exiles severed from their cultural homelands, to write in a mixture of languages was symbolically to undermine the notion (trumpeted by Marinetti) that any one nation had a special claim on culture, that any one language had a prerogative on truth or insight. Given that intention, it is appropriate that the listener should be prevented from paying exclusive attention to any one of the linguistic wavelengths available. The inference is that truth or beauty or insight has rather to be sought in the unexplored gaps between cultures and languages, or in the kind of eclectically hybrid idiom which Ball experiments with in 'Gadji beri bimba'.

More fundamentally, beyond these politico-cultural agendas of anti-militarism or internationalism, the text, despite its playful aspects, raises the spectre of a despairing of language altogether, as it enacts a testing of European language possibilities to the point of destruction. The fear was that language, the poet's raw material, had become irreversibly debased by cheap rhetoric or advertising patter. The alarming notion that the resources of a lingua franca might be so discredited that the individual, even the poet, is incapable of renewing them, leads to experiments in dismantling the substance of language itself—writing nonsense lines, or lettrist poems which have sound but no sense, or juxtaposing speech with mechanical noise to suggest the exhaustion of meaning. Such procedures can however carry a positive as well as a negative charge: they can bespeak not only a despair of prevailing language but a corresponding and profound need to find elsewhere, in non-verbal or pre-linguistic elements, the building bricks of new forms of expression. So the less prestigious linguistic forms come to the fore—children's babble, onomatopoeia, wordless chant, the language of 'savages'. Those new forms of expression are, however, open, multiple, constantly under negotiation and reconstruction, as (*mutatis mutandis*) in Rimbaud's *Illuminations*; the building bricks are never allowed to complete a building—rhythm manifests itself always as process, and never as conclusive.

In the Zurich Dada project, however, rhythmic experimentation is fundamental. From the unforgiving trochaic beat of 'Capriccio' to the unpredictable cross-rhythms of the 'poème simultan' the range is great, and reflects the double-edged vocation of the avant-garde to dismantle the old and to create something wholly new. Thus the drumbeat of a single pulse, for all its ambivalence, is deployed in the main as an instrument of aggression directed against the compromised refinements of contemporary poetics. 'Gadji', however, in its freestanding detachment from ideology or from any national linguistic culture, provides for Ball a created space of cultural and linguistic autonomy which permits him to deploy patterns of simple dactylic and trochaic rhythms as a powerful structuring element without reference to a compromised cultural tradition. In the multivocality of 'L'Amiral' the rhythmic effects become still more aleatory, being open to considerable variation in performance. The complex layering includes counterpoint between languages, between speech and song, between 'poetic' and 'prosaic' utterance and between verbal and non-verbal sound. As in 'Gadji' the parallel texts intermittently exploit conventional metrical patterns. Rhythm is again being liberated in a textual and sonic space beyond anything that the earlier exponents of 'vers libre' might have imagined, generating unforeseen effects in a semi-improvised medium of language and sound. While the texts aggressively or sarcastically evoke apocalypse, decadence or triviality, the creativity in performance depends on a rhythmic kaleidoscope drawing on high and low culture, reassembled afresh in each performance. In their quite different ways, 'Gadji' and 'l'Amiral' both enact an uprooting of rhythm from its national or ideological setting and a redeployment of its most basic elements in a new interlingual or multi-authored space, which creatively represents the internationalist and anti-authoritarian convictions of Zurich Dada. 'Karawane' and 'Gadji' may seem to end in sounds of muffled bathos, and the simultaneous voices tell us that the Admiral has found nothing — but the provocative inventiveness of the texts themselves is the product of an extraordinary imaginative quest in which rhythm is all-important.

NOTES

1   Tristan Tzara, 'Manifeste Dada 1918', in *Œuvres complètes* (Paris: Flammarion, 1975–91) I, 359–67 (362–3) (hereafter *OC*). Translations are my own unless otherwise indicated.

2   As another member of Zurich Dada, Hugo Ball, wrote on 12 March 1916: 'What we are celebrating is both a piece of buffoonery and a requiem mass' (*Die Flucht aus der Zeit* (Zurich: Limmat, 1992), 86). This invaluable text has

been translated as *Flight out of time: a Dada diary,* edited by John Elderfield and translated by Ann Raimes (Berkeley: University of California Press, 1995), but the translations I give here are sometimes worded differently.

3 Richard Huelsenbeck, 'Erste Dadarede in Deutschland', in *Dada Almanach,* edited by R. Huelsenbeck (Berlin: Erich Reiss Verlag, 1920; reprinted New York: Something Else Press, 1966), 104–8 (105–6).

4 Tzara, *OC* I, 75–84. For H. Béhar's notes on the text, see 639.

5 See Isabelle Krzywkowski, *Le Temps et l'espace sont morts hier. Les années 1910–1920: Poésie et poétique de la première avant-garde* (Paris: L'Improviste, 2006), 91. The Futurists' convictions and practices in these regards were also taken up by Pierre-Albert Birot and the 'SIC' group in Paris.

6 'Deutschland über alles', *SIC* 13 (January 1917) (reprint of journal: Paris: Jean-Michel Place, 1980, 98).

7 F.T. Marinetti et al., 'Sintesi futurista della guerra' (20 September 1914), in Marinetti, *Teoria e invenzione futurista* (Milan: Mondadori, 1968), 326–7.

8 Ball, *Flucht aus der Zeit,* 89.

9 Ball, *Flucht aus der Zeit,* 86.

10 Tzara, 'Note sur la poésie' (1919), in *OC* I, 403–5 (404).

11 Richard Huelsenbeck, 'Capriccio', in *Die Aktion,* 9/10 (March 1916) (reprint Munich, Kösel-Verlag, 1967, 123). The full heading of the poem is 'Capriccio/ Nach der strammen "Sturm-Methode" gedichtet', indicating that the text is emulating the percussive style of the poet August Stramm (1874–1915) who published regularly in the Expressionist periodical *Der Sturm.* Stramm's long poem 'Die Menschheit', dating from July 1914 and published in *Der Sturm* in November 1916, deploys this trochaic rhythm and persistent alliteration relentlessly for several hundred lines.

12 Translation of such an alliterative text where sound and rhythm trump sense is of course highly problematic. In context 'klammen' sounds as though it should be a verb, but if so it is not listed, though 'klamm' as an adjective can mean 'clammy', hence my 'clamming'. 'Klauben' is in use in Switzerland, Austria and S. Germany to mean, most often, to 'pick up', 'pick out' or 'gather'. 'Bimmel' is a bell; 'Baumel' is not given as a noun, but the verb 'baumeln' means 'dangle'; 'Bummel' is a stroll.

13 Text (in German) reproduced in Richard Huelsenbeck, *Memoirs of a Dadaist Drummer* (Berkeley: University of California Press, 1974), 62. He claims in these *Memoirs* that the text was 'making fun' of 'the primitives' who had abandoned comprehensibility — but the reflections in this whole account, drafted fifty years after the event and written with a conservative American audience in mind, appear to show some judicious reinterpretation of his own motives as a Dadaist.

14 Ball, 'Karawane', *Gesammelte Gedichte* (Zurich: Die Arche, 1963), 28.

15 Ball, *Flucht aus der Zeit,* 105–6.

16 For closer analysis of the vocabulary used in Ball's sound-poems and observations on their significance, see Rex Last, *German Dadaist Literature: Kurt Schwitters, Hugo Ball, Hans Arp* (New York: Twayne, 1973), 89–97.

17 Ball, 'Gadji beri bimba', *Gesammelte Gedichte*, 27.

18 A view of these sound-poems as related to mystical 'speaking in tongues' is explored by Leonard Forster, 'Poetry of significant nonsense', *Revue de l'Association pour l'étude du mouvement Dada* 1 (October 1965), 22–32.

19 Ball wrote of his own performance: 'The stresses became heavier, the expression became more intense with the sharpening of the consonants' (*Flucht aus der Zeit*, 105).

20 'L'amiral cherche une maison à louer. Poème simultan par R. Huelsenbeck, M. Janko, Tr. Tzara', in Tzara, *OC* I, 492–3. Tzara appends to the text an ironic, name-dropping 'Note pour les bourgeois', in which he sets out an artistic pedigree for this 'modern aesthetic', referring among others to Picasso, Villiers de l'Isle-Adam, Mallarmé, Marinetti, Apollinaire and particularly to Henri Barzun's theoretical work *Voix, rythmes et chants simultanés* (1913), which advocated a simultaneist poetry orchestrating different strands. Barzun regarded rhythm as a basic common factor in human creativity.

21 'Il déshabilla sa chair' appears to echo the line 'il va déboutonner dans son corps de sang la chair qui m'appelle' (He will unbutton in his body of blood the flesh which calls out to me) from 'Tristesse domestique' (*OC* I, 43), and the lighthouse with its circling birds, the shitting archangels and the train like a wounded animal are all lifted from the poem 'Tourne autour' (*OC* I, 59). Tzara would seem to be dismantling his own past work, as well as European culture. These early works were published in Rumanian only in 1934, and in French not until 1965.

22 As Cornelius Partsch suggests, 'The performance [of 'L'Amiral'] both acts out the violence of the prevailing order and offers an alternative to its own destructive logic'. See Partsch, 'The mysterious moment: early Dada performance as ritual' in *Dada Culture. Critical texts of the Avant-garde*, edited by Dafydd Jones (Amsterdam: Rodopi, 2006), 37–65 (49).

Finding Rhythm in Julio Cortázar's *Los Premios*

PETER DAYAN AND CAROLINA ORLOFF

Abstract:
One character in Cortázar's novel (Persio) truly believes in cosmic rhythm. This belief is characteristic of a magical view of the universe central to 1960s (proto-'New Age') counterculture. The other characters in *Los Premios*, like the implied narrator, reject Persio's essentialism; they dismiss the notion that there is really any rhythm common to art, humanity, and the universe. However, there are key points in the narrative, inspired by falling in love and by works of art, at which their world does appear patterned by just such a rhythm, a '*swing cósmico*'. The novel itself turns out to depend on the intermittent conviction of this rhythm, not objectively embedded in anything, but always seen, living, and dying in time; the price of art is the acceptance of this rhythmed mortality.

Keywords: rhythm, Cortázar, *Los Premios*, Pauwels and Bergier, swing, essentialism

On the surface, *Los Premios* (*The Winners*) is a novel with a rather neat circular structure. It begins with a prologue, which recounts how its protagonists, prize-winners in a state-sponsored lottery, come together in a Buenos Aires bar called the *London*, and are taken on board the *Malcolm*, a peculiar vessel described as a 'barco mixto' (mixed boat),[1] built to carry both passengers and freight. The *Malcolm*, they have been told, is to take them on a cruise lasting three or four months; this cruise is their lottery prize. Three sections follow, entitled 'Primer Día', 'Segundo Día' and 'Tercer Día' (Day One, Day Two and Day Three), which recount the three days they actually spend on the ship. And an 'Epílogo' returns the prize-winners to Buenos Aires (on seaplanes). The last sentence of the book has three of them heading back to the *London*, the bar where it all started.

The whole novel is divided into 45 numbered chapters, in which the action is recounted by an extradiegetic third-person narrator. At irregular intervals, interspersed among those 45 chapters, are nine chapters in italics, identified by the letters A to I. These italic chapters seem to be based around the meditations of one of the characters,

Paragraph 33:2 (2010) 215–229
DOI: 10.3366/E0264833410000854

Persio, increasingly mingled, in a curious kind of third-person free indirect discourse, with the reflections of the narrator. It is principally in and around those nine chapters that the concept of rhythm is explicitly discussed. But as we shall see, the problems of rhythm contaminate the whole novel — before, perhaps, justifying it.

***

It is not difficult to surmise why Persio should be given his own separate set of chapters. He does not think in the same way as the other adult characters. For them, there are two main forces, two types of causality, that determine the course of events, and of human behaviour in general. The first of these controlling instances is authority, represented principally by the rather sinister and faceless authority of the Argentinian state, backed up by physical force. Half the passengers on the *Malcolm* accept and approve of this authority. Others, though (including the book's virile masculine heroes), refuse authority when it tries to constrain them; they perceive it as an affront to their human dignity, and rebel. Their rebellion splits the passengers on the *Malcolm* into two camps. The anti-authoritarians set out to defy an incomprehensible prohibition on visiting the stern of the ship. This determines the catastrophe, in which one of the anti-authoritarians is shot by the crew, and all the remaining passengers are forcibly repatriated. We never discover why the state was so anxious to keep the passengers away from the stern of the *Malcolm*; those who went there found nothing, which seems to symbolize the general inscrutability and pointlessness of authority as it appears in the book.

The other motor of human behaviour, the other type of causality for all the characters except Persio, is the most traditional of all in novels: it is the search for love. It is no coincidence that the characters opposed to authority are also those who are responsible for the more interesting and original amorous encounters in the work. Characters who accept authority seem devoid of libido, or at best saddled with a boringly predictable one, of limited use for the novelist.

Persio, however, seems to stand apart from both kinds of fray. About the authority of the state and of the ship's officers, he has nothing to say. He takes no part in the forming and dissolving of liaisons that goes on at vertiginous speed between the passengers (not to mention between one adolescent male passenger and a very large crew member). Persio seems to have his own separate way of seeing the world, in which love, like authority, is only one way of forming patterns among many, all interconnected. What interests him is, indeed, patterns; but only to the extent that he can see them as rhythms.

The first time that the word 'ritmo' (rhythm) occurs in the work, it is pronounced by Persio, in conversation with his friend Claudia. Claudia is an eminently sensible person, as well as highly intelligent and cultured; she is therefore able to put Persio's way of thinking in context, to point out how abnormal it is. Persio has been imagining humanity as an enormous centipede, of which each human individual would be a leg, or perhaps a segment. Claudia is clearly sceptical of the coherence, the totalisation of humanity, implied by this image. Persio is willing to admit that the centipede of humanity may not always hold together; but he is less willing to abandon hope that there may be something essential in its life pattern. Clinging to his invertebrate image, he continues:

Lo que me gustaría averiguar (. . .) es si el ciempiés humano responde a algo más que el azar en su constitución y si disolución; si es una figura, en un sentido mágico, y si esa figura es capaz de moverse bajo ciertas circunstancias en planos más esenciales que los de sus miembros aislados. Uf.

— ¿Más esenciales? — dijo Claudia —. Veamos primero ese vocabulario sospechoso. (45, ch. 10)

('What I would like to find out (. . .) is whether the human centipede, in its constitution and its dissolution, corresponds to something other than chance; whether it is a figure, in the magical sense of the word, and whether that figure is able to move, under certain circumstances, in more essential planes than those of its individual parts. Oof.'

'More essential?' said Claudia. 'Let us first of all examine this suspect vocabulary.')

Persio appears to ignore Claudia's invitation to question his essentialism. He carries on talking in essentialist mode, without trying to justify it rationally. At the same time, though, he attempts to override Claudia's objection by replacing 'I' with 'we' in his presentation of the essentialist viewpoint. His aim is to draw her in by implying that, while he may be the only one who dares to speak of the essential, we all, in practice, behave as if we believed in it; and the mark of this belief is our sense of rhythm:

— Cuando miramos una constelación — dijo Persio — tenemos algo así como una seguridad de que el acorde, el ritmo que une sus estrellas, y que ponemos nosotros, claro, pero que ponemos porque también allí pasa algo que determina ese acorde, es más hondo, más sustancial que la presencia aislada de sus estrellas. (45, ch. 10)

('When we look at a constellation', said Persio, 'we get a certain feeling of confidence that the harmony, the rhythm joining the stars (a rhythm which is imposed by us, of course, yet this imposition occurs because something else also happens out there which determines this harmony), that rhythm is more profound, more substantial than the individual presence of each of its stars.')

This, in the novel, appears at the time less than half convincing, or at best an archaism. Only Persio spends a significant amount of time looking at the stars. Only he really seems to care about the rhythm of the constellations, and to believe that if we perceive such a rhythm in the stars, it cannot simply be a projection of our own human imagination, but must be connected with something that is genuinely happening outside us, 'allí' (out there). His obscure quasi-astrological way of thinking marks him out as a 'mago de verdad' (95, ch. 17) (true magician), a 'todolosabe' (144, ch. 23) (visionary), a believer in some kind of occult truth, for which the action of the novel gives no evidence, and which none of the other adult characters takes at all seriously. Does that mean that we have no reason to take seriously the notion of rhythm, since its principal proponent in the novel seems out of tune with the novel's true causality? Is it not an outdated notion, from the childhood of humanity? To answer this question, one has to separate out the world depicted in the novel from the novel itself. Literature must be distinguished from reality; the causal principles of art must be pried away from those of the material world.

Los Premios portrays a certain Argentinian social reality of the 1950s. As we have seen, the members of that society divide quite neatly into two camps: those who have faith in authority, and the anti-authoritarians. The latter firmly believe that there is no essential or divine order governing the stars, nature, humanity, history, politics, society in general, art in general, or poetry. In accordance with this rejection of essential order, the anti-authoritarians have no time for Persio's idea of a universal rhythm pervading the cosmos. For them, the state of nature is characterised by a rhythmless macrocosmic disorder which mirrors the microcosmic disorder they see within themselves. Carlos López, for example, one of the leaders of the anti-authoritarian lottery winners, is presented to us from the very first chapter as a sceptic in all matters metaphysical. His native tendency is to believe that no purposefully ordained order exists in the world, within him or without. He opposes his world view to that of his colleague Restelli, a pro-authoritarian who always supports the state's power:

—Admiro su confianza en el orden burocrático—dijo López —. Se ve que
corresponde al orden interno de su persona, por decirlo así. Yo en cambio soy
como valija de turco y nunca estoy seguro de nada. (16, ch. 1)

('I admire your faith in the bureaucratic order,' said López. 'It seems to match your
own internal order, if I may put it like that. I, on the other hand, am like a dog's
breakfast and am never sure about anything.')

But as Carlos López falls in love, with the novel's red-haired 'femme
fatale', Paula Lavalle, there is a curious gradual erosion of this
scepticism. A certain order, or at least a certain unity, appears in the
way López sees the world; and that order is described as essentially
rhythmic. In fact, the more Carlos López falls in love, the more
closely his thought patterns come to resemble Persio's. This increasing
resemblance then contaminates the narrative voice itself, until a
crisis point is reached at which the narrative voice acknowledges a
temporary inability to distinguish between Persio and López—and
between them and itself.

  The agent, the vector, one might almost say the virus that infects
López and the narrator with Persio's sense of rhythm is a cubist
painting by Picasso of a guitarist. We are repeatedly told that it
belonged to Apollinaire (author, we may remind ourselves, of 'La Jolie
Rousse' ('The Pretty Redhead')). That painting is mentioned in six
of Persio's nine italic chapters. It fascinates him. In its theme and in
its construction, it seems to represent that ambiguous, unsettled, never
discovered musicality which he seeks but can never quite convincingly
locate in the physical world. In chapter 33, as López falls in love, the
image of the cubist guitar strangely comes to suffuse the discourse of
López and the narrator. It superimposes itself on what they think and
see; so that we gradually we find that guitar, the *Malcolm*, and Paula's
red hair blending into a single image, as music, painting, magic, the
voyage, and the process of falling in love are identified as all similar,
precisely in that they all share a certain kind of rhythm: a rhythm
identified as *swing*.

  Swing, for Cortázar, whose tastes in jazz were not dissimilar
from those of Jacques Réda (see Eric Prieto's essay in this volume),
represents, as it does for Réda, a kind of rhythm which is neither purely
improvised and personal, nor formally determined by convention. It
comes to life through an undecidable interchange between individual
inspiration, and an unsayable pattern located irredeemably beyond
the individual. It is perceived as if it were a property of the whole
universe; and yet at the same time, its perceptible presence depends

on something that properly belongs to, and emanates from, a single person. For López, the connection between the personal and the cosmic, the wire along which the cosmic swing transmits to him its electricity, is figured by Paula Lavalle's red hair:

cada cabello una zarza ardiente, hilo eléctrico por el que corre el fluido que mueve el *Malcolm* y las máquinas del mundo, la acción de los hombres y la derrota de las galaxias, el absolutamente indecible *swing* cósmico en este primer cabello (el observador no alcanza a despegarse de él (. . .)). (275, ch, 33)

(every filament of hair is a burning briar, an electric thread carrying the fluid which moves the *Malcolm* and all the machines of the world, the action of men and the rout of galaxies, the utterly unsayable cosmic *swing* in this first filament of hair (the observer cannot quite detach himself from it (. . .)).)

This vision is unmistakably Persio-esque in its perception of a single unifying essential fluid, a central rhythm reaching us from the stars, a cosmic swing running through everything from a single hair to the movement of the galaxies. López, we might think, the metaphysical sceptic, would surely not see the world thus. And yet the fascination with Paula's hair is equally unmistakably López's, not Persio's. Who, then, is here 'el observador'? In intradiegetic terms, as the narrator subsequently says, López is the most likely suspect. But it might almost as well be the narrator himself; and the blurring of distinctions, at precisely this point in the novel, between the voices of López, of Persio, and of the narrator, extends to the viewpoint of the reader, who is, after all, an observer of the whole scene. It is this process of blurring and extension, this loss of the observer's ability to detach himself, that allows rhythm, philosophically confined to Persio, to become catching; and it is in turn as rhythm becomes catching that literature, in the terms of this novel, is born. In other words: López, as he falls in love, feels the rhythm; he cannot speak it (it is, and we will return to this point, unsayable, properly 'indecible'), nor can he believe in it, as might Persio, as an objective property of the universe; but Julio Cortázar can share with him, with Persio, and with us the development of his sense of that rhythm as something musical, spreading outwards from Paula's hair as love re-organizes his world.

Every rhythm is a coming and going; and in the next sentence, the points of view of Persio, López, and the narrator appear once again to diverge — or do they?

Y al mismo tiempo todo es como una guitarra (pero si Persio estuviera aquí proclamaría la guitarra negándose al término de comparación (. . .) sin permitir que se empleara como juego metafórico, de donde cabe inferir que quizá Carlos López es agente y paciente de estas visiones (...)) resumiendo, todo es una guitarra desde arriba (...). (276, ch. 33)

(And at the same time everything is like a guitar (yet, if Persio were here he would proclaim the guitar while denying the term of comparison (...), not allowing the guitar to be used as a metaphorical game, from which it can be inferred that perhaps Carlos López is both agent and recipient of these visions (...)) to conclude, everything is a guitar from above (...).)

This is peculiar. The narrator first says that everything is *like* a guitar; he implies that only the mystically inclined Persio would go so far as to maintain that analogy is indistinguishable from identity, thus collapsing the metaphor. But one sentence later, the narrator apparently adopts Persio's voice, and tells us that, seen from above, everything *is* a guitar. And he continues with his collapsed metaphor of the world-guitar, speaking like Persio, and not like the more normal characters, represented here by López:

la mano del guitarrista posada en los trastes sin que la señora de Trejo, repantigada en una mecedora verde, sepa que ella es esa mano cruzada y agazapada en los trastes, y la otra mano es el mar encendido a babor, rascando el flanco de la guitarra como los gitanos cuando esperan o pausan un tiempo de cante, el mar como lo sintió Picasso cuando pintaba el hombre de la guitarra que fue de Apollinaire. (276, ch. 33)

(the guitarist's hand rests on the frets, without Señora Trejo, reclining on a green sunlounger, knowing that she is that hand crossing and clutching the frets, and the other hand is the sea in flames to port, scratching the guitar's flank as gypsies do when they hold or pause a song's time, the sea as Picasso felt it when he painted the man with the guitar, which belonged to Apollinaire.)

Our narrator seems, here, to be losing touch with reality. How can he certify that as he painted the guitarist, Picasso really did feel the sea as the right hand of a gypsy guitarist? But this, while it might be a reason for doubting his critical sense (one would not be entitled to make such an affirmation in an academic article), is a pointer towards the continuing transformation of his voice; precisely the same transformation as the one that turns the sea into the source of a musical temporality. In the novel, rhythm, the time of music, appears only as the voice loses critical distance.

Literature can only present rhythm as if it were somewhere in the world, not only represented in the world but actually emerging from the world. In fact, this is an illusion. Rhythm has no fixed or stable presence in the world; even Persio eventually senses this. Its instability is made tangible in its dependence on point of view. Rhythm is seen, felt, believed in, and then again not seen; it always depends on an angle of vision. To rub this point in, the narrator gives us his image of the world as a guitar, seen from above, and then tells us that López, who is on the ship, cannot see it thus. Continuing the quotation from where we left off:

Y esto ya no puede estarlo pensando Carlos López, pero es Carlos López el que junto a Paula pierde los ojos en uno solo de sus cabellos y siente vibrar un instrumento en la confusa instancia de fuerzas que es toda cabellera, el entrecruzamiento potencial de miles y miles de cabellos, cada uno la cuerda de un instrumento sigiloso que se tendería sobre kilómetros de mar, un arpa como el arpamujer de Jerónimo Bosch, en suma otra guitarra antepasada, en suma una misma música que llena la boca de Carlos López de un profundo gusto a frutillas y a cansancio y a palabras. (276, ch. 33)

(And it cannot any longer be Carlos López thinking this, but it is Carlos López who, next to Paula, loses his eyes in a single strand of her hair, who feels an instrument vibrate in the confused pleading of forces made entirely of hair, the potential interlacing of thousands and thousands of hairs, each one the string of a secret instrument extending over miles of sea, a harp like Hieronymus Bosch's harp-woman, in sum another preceding guitar, in sum a single music which fills Carlos López's mouth with a deep taste of strawberries, of fatigue and of words.)

Hair expands to become the strings of a musical instrument. That hair-strung musical instrument maps itself first onto the material world, netting the ocean, and then onto the representation of music in art. In both cases, what is emphasized is not the thing, not what is really there, but the force of a vision. That is what gives us music. And it is that music which in turn fills the mouth of Carlos López with a taste of (among other things) words. Not the words of the sceptic, which have no such taste and are not born of (or borne by) music, but the words of which love or a novel can be made.

   Music, then, once we have managed to see it as a property of the world, gives a taste of the words that can become art. And yet we had been told, but a page earlier, that the 'swing cósmico' was 'absolutamente indecible': beyond words. Is there a contradiction here? Not really. The 'swing cósmico' does indeed remain properly unsayable. It is not the rhythm itself that words can express; it is the matter in which we see it incarnated. Persio and Carlos López do not see the 'swing cósmico' itself. The former sees a guitar, the latter sees Paula's hair. It is these objects of vision which, apparently, to the mind of the character or of the narrator (but let us remember that not all the people on the *Malcolm* would share this vision), contain it. For the writer, it is the hair, the hair and the movement of expansion that allows it to transmit the '*swing* cósmico', which can and do give rise to words — as will the inevitable subsequent contraction, when hair becomes once again mere hair.

***

Three years after *Los Premios*, Cortázar published *Rayuela* (*Hopscotch*), which has remained, doubtless, his most celebrated novel. One of its characters is an experimental writer, Morelli, who speaks of what swing means to him. Morelli's views on the subject echo and amplify those we have found in *Los Premios*. The reactions of other characters to Morelli's writing pose with peculiar acuteness the question of where rhythm can be located. Furthermore, Cortázar gives that question a clear context in the history of ideas, in a way that he could not have done (as we shall see) in *Los Premios*. So we will allow ourselves an excursion through *Rayuela*, to profit from the clarification it affords on these matters, before returning to the earlier work.

A number of chapters, in *Rayuela*, are in Morelli's voice. He describes how he writes. It is clear that, like Mallarmé (to whom he is explicitly compared),[2] writing, for him, cannot be justified by an idea to be communicated. Rather, it must do something which can only be initially evoked by analogy with music — or more precisely, with rhythm:

¿Por qué escribo esto? No tengo ideas claras, ni siquiera tengo ideas. Hay jirones, impulsos, bloques, y todo busca una forma, entonces entra en juego el ritmo y yo escribo dentro de ese ritmo, escribo por él, movido por él (...) el *swing*, un balanceo rítmico (...) ese *swing* en el que se va informando la materia confusa, es para mí la única certidumbre de su necesidad, porque apenas cesa comprendo que no tengo ya nada que decir.[3]

(Why I am writing this? I have no clear ideas, I do not even have ideas.[4] There are tugs, impulses, blocks and everything is looking for a form, then rhythm comes into play and I write within that rhythm, I write by it, moved by it (...) the *swing* begins at once, a rhythmic swaying (...) this *swing* in which confused material goes about taking shape, is for me the only certainty of its necessity, because no sooner does it stop than I understand that I no longer have anything to say.)

Morelli knows that when writing is not governed by rhythm, it ceases to be of any value; without rhythm, the writer has nothing to say. He also knows that he cannot actively decide or determine its presence; he cannot calculate it. Rhythm seems to determine itself, to come before his words. In this, Morelli's sense of the order of events, for the writer, corresponds to that of Valéry and Woolf, as analysed by David Evans and Emma Sutton in this volume. Morelli does not create rhythm; rather, he is moved by it. This sense of a certain lack of control, of initiative abandoned, is at the very core of his values as a writer. The question is: to what does he abandon himself? Where can one locate that rhythm which inspires him?

Some of his readers have a clear answer to this question: it is in the deep structures of the universe. Wong, one of Morelli's admirers, maintains that there is actually no point in making the effort to read Morelli's complex writings; all one needs to do is to read two quotations found among Morelli's papers which, positing the existence of 'estructuras profundas' (profound structures) inaccessible to positivist binary thought, end with an appeal for a new state of mind with a new kind of thinking:

sería necesario que otras máquinas que las usuales se pusieran a funcionar en el cerebro, que el razonamiento binario fuese sustituido por una conciencia analógica que asumiera las formas y asimilara los ritmos inconcebibles de esas estructuras profundas.[5]

(other machinery than that normally in use would have to be started up in the brain, whose binary system of reasoning would have to be replaced by an analogical consciousness which would assume the form, and assimilate the inconceivable rhythms of these profound structures.)

The quotation Wong gives us here (with no indication of what Morelli might have said about it) is translated from *Le Matin des magiciens: introduction au réalisme fantastique* (*The Morning of the Magicians: an introduction to fantastic realism*) by Pauwels and Bergier, first published in 1960.[6] This book, a best-selling cult classic in its time, reads today like a remarkable foreshadowing of '60s alternative culture. It draws parallels between the conceptual difficulty of quantum physics, and the problems of believing in alchemy, magic, prophesy, poetry, and paranormal phenomena. Quoting Pauli as readily as Rimbaud, regarding William Blake as inspired in the same sense that Einstein was, Pauwels and Bergier encourage us to believe in a single fantastic reality behind science, art, and the great religious and esoteric traditions of the past, a reality that unifies all higher human experience and understanding. The unity of that reality is metaphorically expressed (though Pauwels and Bergier do not attempt to explain the metaphor) in musical terms. They wonder, for example, 'why it is that poets have not yet turned to science to catch an echo of the music of these spheres of fantastic reality' (237).

It is that word 'reality' (echoed in the book's subtitle) which conveys the fundamental difference between two views of rhythm: that shared by Wong, Pauwels, Bergier, and (so we will argue) Persio; and that of Morelli and of the narrator in *Los Premios*. For Pauwels and Bergier, the 'music of the spheres' actually exists, as a reality, albeit fantastic; we may not always have ears to hear it, but the 'rhythms' of the 'profound structures' are always there, immanent in the universe. If that is the case, in the end, no writing is necessary; what matters is the music that exists beyond it. Hence Wong's principle that one does not need to read Morelli's books, but only to understand what he is telling us — which Pauwels and Bergier had said before him. The 'swing' of Morelli, however, like that of the narrator of *Los Premios*, does not have the character of a reality. It is not encoded in the universe. Science has no access to it. It has no stable existence. It comes and goes; and its coming and going is not merely a function of our ability to appreciate something that was always there. Rhythm, though it is felt by the writer to precede his words, actually lives and dies with those words. For Wong, the text can be dispensed with, once one has understood its message about the situation of rhythm. For Morelli, on the contrary, it is the text, not the message, that matters.

The Morning of the Magicians is, as we have seen, an important reference point in *Rayuela*. However, Cortázar cannot have read it before he wrote *Los Premios*; both books were published in 1960, but he had finished writing *Los Premios* in 1958. The similarities between Persio's beliefs and those of Pauwels and Bergier are all the more striking. It is impossible, indeed, not to think that Cortázar must have been struck, when he read *The Morning of the Magicians*, by the extent to which he had himself foreseen not only its key arguments, but also the difficulties that they fail to address. Like Pauwels and Bergier, Persio seeks a deeper reality through the wisdom both of science and of astrological tradition. He hears the music of the spheres as they do. He senses rhythm in profound, hidden structures, just as they do. He shares their difficulty in finding those structures in contemporary poetry. And he also shares their conviction that the profound structures are present in the material world as well as the spiritual. Chapter F of *Los Premios*, the last of the section entitled 'First Day', is the chapter that most explicitly gives voice to this conviction. It is here that Persio begins to describe how he imagines he might have experienced a sense of identification with the music of the universe, by embracing physically the soil of Argentina. In the process, he rejects all that words can do. Does one need poetry?

¿ (...) esa proxeneta de la hermosura, de la euforia, de los finales felices, de tanta prostitución encuadernada en tela y explicada en los institutos de estilística? No, no quiero poesía inteligible a bordo, ni tampoco voodoo o ritos iniciáticos. Otra cosa más inmediata, menos copulable por la palabra, algo libre de tradición para que por fin lo que toda tradición enmascara surja como un alfanje de plutonio a través de un biombo lleno de historias pintadas. Tirado en la alfalfa pude ingresar en ese orden, aprender sus formas, porque no serán palabras sino ritmos puros (...) (264, ch. F)

(that pimp of beauty, of euphoria, of happy endings, of so much cloth-bound prostitution elucidated in institutes for stylistics? No, I don't want intelligible poetry on board, any more than I want voodoo or initiation rites. Rather, something else, more immediate, that words cannot copulate with, something free of tradition so that at last, that which all tradition conceals might emerge like a plutonium cutlass through a screen covered with painted stories. Laying down on the alfalfa, I could enter this order, learn its forms, because these are not words but pure rhythms (...).)

We should not be surprised, certainly, by Persio's rejection of words. It aligns him with the rejection by Pauwels and Bergier of the binary system of reasoning which they identify with the rationality of human language. Like them, Persio believes in the existence of a magical rhythm hidden, yet essentially present, in the material world;[7] a rhythm whose logic is foreign to that of words, and which one can only appreciate when language is silenced. We have seen how Wong, in *Rayuela*, considers Morelli's actual writings as potentially superfluous: once one has understood the point he is trying to make (which is that what really matters is not what words can do, but a rhythm in the universe that words obscure), words themselves become unnecessary. Literature itself, at this point, turns into a veil whose true function is to be cast aside. Persio shares this conviction. He, too, feels that poetry exists to be cast aside in favour of something more essential. However, he is alone in *Los Premios* in this belief.

To Persio, a pure rhythm exists, of itself, as the form of an order into which one ought of right to be able to enter, even if only in privileged moments. It exists before language, before music as we make it, before any representation. None of the other characters shares his faith in the prior and real existence of such a rhythm. To them, as, one suspects, to Cortázar, Persio's alternative between 'palabras' and 'ritmos puros' is a false one; false, not because words can be pure rhythm, but because pure rhythm does not exist. Rhythm is always already impure, always impurely incarnated, and always experienced impurely. Is it beyond words as it is beyond love? The question is as false as Persio's alternative; for it is only through words, or through falling in love, that we find rhythm in the novel; without such experiences, including their instability in time, it does not exist. Indeed, it is this very peculiar position, of something perceived *through* yet always as though it were *beyond*, that explains the persistence of the word 'rhythm', with its musical implications.

In the great Mallarmean tradition to which Cortázar, like Morelli, belongs, music, within literature, represents that quality of art which is not merely an expression of what exists. It has a disturbing dual relationship with the writer's words: it has no objective existence without them, yet it is experienced always as beyond, indeed prior to, those words. Does it exist, or is it a mere illusion? To that question, the answer must remain unstable. Music itself, the music of voices or of guitars, certainly does exist, as sound events in time; just as words exist as marks upon a page. However, the true essence of art is always something, not present, but sensed, imagined, or felt beyond the real existence even of music. In *Los Premios*, it is this essence, to be sought, in literature, in the same direction as music, but further away still, outside even music's physical manifestations, that voices other than Persio's voice experience as rhythm. They need not share Persio's rejection of poetry. To them as to him, the words of poetry are impure; but for them, that impurity is a necessary ingredient of our experience of rhythm, in any art form. The true temporality of rhythm in the art of their time is given by the way it appears alternately present in, and absent from, the material; whether that material be words on a page, the sound of music, painting, the hair of the beloved, a constellation, or the land and skyscapes of the motherland.

Claudia's suspicion of Persio's essentialism is justified to the extent that Persio looks for rhythm in the human centipede, or in the Argentinian pampas, as if it should always be there. It cannot always be anywhere, not even in music. There is no way to capture it, to pin it down, by any definition or means of analysis; its presence always depends on a vision that appears, from points of view that only lunatics can constantly avoid, an illusion. Nothing stably contains it; we cannot enter it. It remains nonetheless a general truth that a music-lover can at times feel convinced it really is there, in music; a lover may see it in a single hair; a reader may sense it in a poem; and Julio Cortázar as novelist may allow his voice to become contaminated with that conviction, enough to let us share it, provided that he is able to allow it repeatedly to be born and to die. That mortality, felt by all his heroes and narrators, is both the uniquely universal characteristic of rhythm, which depends on birth and death in time, and the true price of rhythm in the novel. It alone permits the modern writer to be honest, both about the imaginary rhythmic origin of his art, and about the peculiarly intermittent character of that truth. Morelli's description of the writing process resembles the birth and death of the '*swing* cósmico' in *Los Premios* in three essentials: the sense of an outside rhythmic force bringing everything into focus; the acceptance that one cannot control that rhythmic force; and the knowledge that, being unconnected with any material, objective truth or reality, that force is destined to die. That instability is a fundamental component of rhythm: it cannot be always there, it is a coming and going, something in it is born, and then dies. Morelli is not alone, in Cortázar's work, in thinking that if one is not brave enough to face that mortality, one should not write — or, indeed, make music.

NOTES

1 Julio Cortázar, *Los Premios* (Madrid: Suma de Letras S.L., 2004). Future references will take the form of the page number followed by the chapter number. A published translation of this novel exists: *The Winners*, translated by Elaine Kerrigan (New York: The New York Review of Books, 1965). Unfortunately, it frequently does not render the aspects of Cortázar's Spanish on which we comment. Therefore, we have provided our own translations.

2 Morelli shares with Mallarmé a sense of terror before the blank sheet of paper, 'un horror mallarmeano frente a la página en blanco' (Julio Cortázar, *Rayuela* (Buenos Aires: Sudamericana, 1963), 442, ch. 99).

3 *Rayuela*, 405, ch. 82. Translation from Julio Cortázar, *Hopscotch*, translated by Gregory Rabassa (New York: Pantheon Books, 1966), 402.

4 Mallarmé more than once said much the same. Most pithily, he describes himself, asked by a journalist what he thinks, responding: 'Justement, je ne pense rien, jamais' (That's the point, I never have thoughts) (Stéphane Mallarmé, 'Solitude', in *Igitur, Divagations, Un Coup de dés* (Paris: Gallimard, 1982), 314).

5 *Rayuela*, 413, ch. 86; *Hopscotch*, 410.

6 Louis Pauwels and Jacques Bergier, *The Morning of the Magicians*, translated by Rollo Myers (London: Souvenir Press, 2001), 236–7.

7   It is the Argentinian pampas, that most sea-like of landscapes, that inspires
    Persio to this rhapsody. Like Dino Campana (see Helen Abbott's essay in this
    volume), Persio finds in the openness and the wide starry skies of the pampas
    a particularly irresistible invitation to sense a rhythm undeniably present in the
    world, yet beyond the scale of human language.

Swung Subjectivity in Jacques Réda

Eric Prieto

Abstract:
This article uses Jacques Réda's theory of poetic swing to show how the traditional metrical analysis of poetic rhythm might be updated to better reflect the rhythmic intricacies of contemporary French literary language. It begins by situating Jacques Réda's rhythmic practices with respect to the deconstructive theories of rhythm and subjectivity espoused by Philippe Lacoue-Labarthe and Henri Meschonnic. Using the concept of swing, Réda seeks to show why certain rhythmic patterns feel 'right' to him, and how they enable him to put his personal stamp on the French language as he seeks to show, like Lacoue-Labarthe and Meschonnic, that there is such a thing as a rhythmic 'essence of the subject'.

Keywords: swing, jazz, *flâneur*, mute 'e', *vers mâché*, walking bass, Meschonnic, Lacoue-Labarthe, Cornulier

Jacques Réda is, in the best sense of the word, a rhythmic poet, one who has made the exploration of rhythmic effects and their role in the production of poetic meaning a central focus of his poetry. In all of his writings on poetic technique, it is the concept of swing, borrowed from jazz, that he uses to explain his conception of rhythmic dynamism. At no time, however, does Réda write poetry that seeks to imitate the rhythmic patterns of the jazz vernacular or to use the kind of hipster diction that the beat poets experimented with. Nor has he sought to set his poetry to music, jazz or otherwise. Indeed, reduced to its core, the term swing as he uses it seems to be essentially a metaphor for rhythmic variability. Why then, apart from a personal affection for the music, does Réda insist so heavily on using this particular term in this particular way? How does it help us to understand what Réda seeks to achieve in both his verse and prose poetry? And what can (his use of) the notion of swing contribute to a more general theory of rhythm and its significance for the literary enterprise? In order to address such questions, we will need to situate his work with respect to the larger debate over rhythm taking place in France in the 1970s and '80s, the period during which he established his distinctive poetic voice.

Paragraph 33:2 (2010) 230–245
DOI: 10.3366/E0264833410000866

The Theory of Rhythm

Metrical verse, as we know, long sat at the aesthetic pinnacle of the language arts. The codified rhythms of metrical verse were conflated with rhythm as a whole and verse provided the measure against which other modes of literature were judged. Since the *crise de vers* evoked by Mallarmé the pre-eminence of verse is no longer assured, but rhythm has remained an important focus of attention. Indeed, as Amittai Aviram has suggested, there seems to have been a decisive resurgence of interest in theorizing rhythm in the 1970s and '80s, particularly in the post-structuralist, deconstructionist milieus of the Parisian intelligentsia.[1] For these thinkers, however, the focus of the interest in rhythm has changed. Rather than treating rhythm in terms of the codified conventions of verse poetry, which implies a high degree of submission to the social order that developed these conventions, they tended to present rhythm as a marker of individuality, indeed, as the bearer of literary subjectivity itself.

Philippe Lacoue-Labarthe's exploration of rhythm provides a useful point of entry into this argument. In one of his major essays, *L'Echo du sujet* (*The Echo of the Subject*), Lacoue-Labarthe uses music, and within music rhythm, as a tool that might, he hopes, enable him to enunciate the principles of a counter-tradition to the rationalist tradition that stretches back through Descartes to Plato.[2] He seeks to show how musical and poetic rhythms might be fundamentally linked to corporeal, psychological, spiritual, and deep 'ontological' rhythms that would provide insights into subjectivity that remain inaccessible to the rationalist tradition and its 'mimetological' definition of subjectivity.[3]

Whatever one may think of this project's overall merits, the strategic role that Lacoue-Labarthe attributes to rhythm leads into a kind of methodological trap, because, as he slowly comes to realize, it relies on shifting definitions of the term rhythm that misleadingly imply synonymy between processes that are related only by analogy. As a result, despite having set out at the beginning of this seventy-page essay to trace the links between music, autobiography, and the theory of the subject, he is ultimately forced to concede that 'it would probably be necessary to dissociate as much as possible the question of rhythm from any musical problematic' (199). This is an admission that throws his initial project — premised on a possible equivalence of musical and ontological rhythms — into disarray.

Of course the task of coming up with a universally valid definition of rhythm is a well-known fool's errand, as David Evans's contribution to the present volume makes clear in relation to Valéry. When writers and critics attempt to explain the significance of poetic rhythms, to show why the detailed study of poetic rhythm might have deeper significance, there is a strong, almost irresistible tendency to seek answers outside the domain of literature. But any explanation of literary rhythms in terms of extra-literary phenomena — be they the pulsations of the human body, the emotional power of music and dance, the psychological patterns that characterize our mental life, the cycles of the seasons, or the harmony of the spheres — introduces levels of mediation that can generate much confusion. That rhythm of all kinds has something to do with recurrence and regularity, as well as variation, fluctuating intensities, and the perception of difference, seems indisputable. But any *operative* (as opposed to speculative, theoretical, or metaphysical) definition of rhythm is going to have, of necessity, domain-specific elements. And although metaphorical applications across disciplinary boundaries are often useful — as a way, for example, to think about unexplored possibilities — they require careful mediation and vigilance, so that we know when we're talking literally and when we're talking metaphorically.[4]

This is one of the great strengths of Henri Meschonnic's monumental *Critique du rythme* (*Critique of rhythm*).[5] Meschonnic, like Lacoue-Labarthe, is conversant with the deconstructive idiom that characterizes much post-structuralist theory, and he shares many of the same concerns, including the often quoted but little explored assertion that there can be no theory of the subject without a theory of rhythm and vice-versa.[6] Unlike Lacoue-Labarthe, however, Meschonnic steadfastly refuses to allow extra-literary definitions of rhythm to interfere with his analyses of verbal texts. He focuses his energy instead on reforming the ways in which rhythm has been dealt with in the tradition of literary criticism. For Meschonnic, who is an active poet and translator (known in particular for his translations of the versets of the Hebrew Bible), our understanding of poetic rhythm has been seriously distorted by the long French tradition of metrical analysis. Meschonnic — rightly, in my opinion — criticizes this tradition for its tendency to treat as rhythmic only those rhythms that can be analysed in terms of the conventions of metrical verse, leading us to undervalue the rhythmic values of irregular verse forms, prose texts, and non-literary discourse of all kinds, including spoken language. This leads Meschonnic to devise an elaborate notational system that seeks to overcome the limitations of traditional metrical analysis by vastly expanding the kinds of events that can be notated while refining the instruments of measurement. Thus, for example, rather than marking only binary oppositions between strong and weak syllables, which is the traditional approach, he tracks multiple levels of stress (indicated by stress markers: ', '', ''', etc.). Moreover, his notational system takes into account many of the semantic, prosodic, and phonological considerations that would have escaped the grasp of a traditional metrical analysis, and is in general more open to the inherent variability of prose rhythms and cognizant of the many kinds of elocutional variation that tend to be ignored in the classical metrical tradition.

If there is a weakness in Meschonnic's approach, it is its very openness. Ultimately, there is no aspect of language that is not rhythmic in his view, which leaves us quickly overwhelmed by the sheer variety of possibilities. (This is a complaint that Benoît de Cornulier, a leading proponent of metrical analysis, levels against all attempts to analyse prose rhythms. The huge variety and variability of prose rhythms makes systematic analysis all but impossible.[7]) Meschonnic is right of course to say that the traditional metrical approach operates according to a reductive understanding of rhythm, and that much of what is interesting in literary prosody is what violates or remains unaccounted for by these norms, but that may be precisely the value of such conventions: to serve as a familiar and widely shared set of rules, a base-line or benchmark, however reductive, against which individualistic gestures can stand out and be measured. Paradoxically, we might say that the greatest limitation of metrical analysis is also its greatest strength: because it excludes so much it is very good at explaining the phenomena it does include. The question is whether these phenomena are the most important ones, given prevailing conditions. And if not, then we need new tools, better adapted to current conditions. This is the imperative that guides Meschonnic's project.

Situating Réda: Swing and subjectivity

Lacoue-Labarthe and Meschonnic will serve here to represent two poles of the post-structuralist discourse on rhythm. Both share a deconstructive, contestatory attitude towards the traditional treatment of rhythm, and a belief in the centrality of rhythm to any viable account of human subjectivity. But whereas Lacoue-Labarthe emphasizes the philosophical history of the concept of rhythm and seeks to use it to deconstruct traditional rationalist conceptions of subjectivity, Meschonnic stresses the empirical dimension of literary rhythms, using his analyses to critique the limiting conventions of metrical analysis, and to emphasize his understanding of subjectivity as a dynamic process.

It is in this context that we can begin to understand Jacques Réda's contribution to the theory and practice of rhythmic analysis. Like Meschonnic, Réda is a conscientious wordsmith who takes care to limit his rhythmic analyses to the verbal level. He also believes, like Lacoue-Labarthe, that there is such a thing as a rhythmic 'essence of the subject' (cf. Lacoue-Labarthe, 167) and has devoted much of his career to exploring the interrelatedness of rhythm and subjectivity posited by Meschonnic. Although he has little to no tolerance for theorists and theory-driven poetry (which he dismisses as 'poésie parlote' [poetry babble]), he feels obligated to understand, explain, and justify his somewhat quirky approach to his art by seeking to discover the underlying principles that explain why certain rhythmic patterns, metrical or otherwise, feel 'right' to him, and what those principles reveal about the possible larger spiritual mission of poetry as he practices it. In this sense we could say that Réda is a mediating figure, one whose ultimate poetic ambitions are metaphysical, but who insists on grounding his explorations of the rhythmic self in the empirical practice of poetry, while also demanding, in rationalist fashion, that all claims about links between the two levels be verifiable.

Walking bass

Réda is best known as a poet of the city, a *flâneur* in the Baudelairean tradition who has devoted himself to writing about his peregrinations in and around Paris, keeping off the beaten track and away from the kinds of monumental locations and pilgrimage points that have traditionally attracted the attention of tourists and poets. He has also led a second career as a jazz critic, writing regularly for *Jazz Magazine* and collecting his writings on jazz in two volumes, *L'improviste* (*Ad lib*) and *Anthologie des musiciens de jazz* (*An Anthology of Jazz Musicians*)[8].

Réda's interest in jazz spills over regularly into his poetry. He routinely borrows titles from jazz compositions, writes of quests to find a coveted album, draws various kinds of analogies between his poetry and the style of his favourite jazzmen, and, most notably, develops his theory of poetic rhythm in dialogue with the music, drawing most heavily on the concept of swing. In *Les Ruines de Paris* (*The Ruins of*

Paris)—a volume composed primarily of prose poems that is still his most widely read collection—one section is titled 'Basse ambulante' (walking bass), a title that combines his interest in the rhythmic feel of jazz with his peripatetic inclinations. The unpremeditated yet attentive wandering of *flânerie* is associated here with the freedom of the improvising musician, while the auditory figure of feet pounding the pavement provides a way for him to connect metaphorically the rhythms of his poetic prose with the vital pulse of the walking bass in jazz.[9]

In *Celle qui vient à pas légers* (*The One Who Comes on Discreet Feet*), a collection of essays in which he attempts to explain and theorize his own poetic practice, he brings the concept of swing to the fore.[10] It provides the prime metaphor for explaining what he is trying to achieve, rhythmically speaking, in both his prose and poetry. Swing, of course, designates the rhythmic feel most widely associated with jazz, and for Réda, the history of jazz begins and ends with swing. His taste in jazz runs to the classical end of the spectrum, from the early hot jazz of Bechet and Armstrong, through Basie and Ellington, Parker, Miles, and early Coltrane, and flirting only tentatively with the work of more 'out' musicians like Eric Dolphy and Albert Ayler. He shows little interest in free jazz or any of the other more radical developments that marked the post-bop phase of jazz history, nor in any of the branches of jazz that broke with the swing feel (fusion, free improvisation, etc.).

In his discussions of jazz, Réda emphasizes the unquantifiable nature of swing, which cannot be exactly notated since it varies from performer to performer and situation to situation and depends more on the intuitive feel of the musicians than on any notatable relationships. Swing is personal. It depends, to be sure, on the established conventions of a shared musical idiom, but opens up an artistic space within which the musician can sculpt his own musical identity. In *Celle qui vient*, his poetic treatise, Réda transfers the concept of swing to the domain of poetry as a way to explain his prosodic experiments and to defend his quirky, playful deployment of rhyme, metre, and verse. He emphasizes in particular the importance of the mute E in French poetry, which he sees as the most important element of any mode of French prosody that seeks to break out of the stilted conventions of traditional metrical verse. Like swung eighth notes, the rhythmic value of the mute E will vary from poet to poet and situation to situation in ways that are all but impossible to predict and quantify. Thus if, for Réda, 'the mute E carries the swing of the French language' (71), it is because 'the mute E is an irrational, non measurable value' (83).

Swing in jazz provides an appropriate analogy for his strategic use of the mute E to the extent that both build on the conventions of classical performance practice, but refuse to adhere strictly to them, preferring instead to play *with* them. Thus Réda writes of swing in terms of 'the secret of a miraculous conflictual equilibrium' (87) and specifies that its interest lies precisely in the tension it creates with respect to the straight rhythms of classical music: 'jazz has carved out its deeply significant rhythmic specificity within the framework of a regularity' (86). In Réda's poetry, this 'miraculous conflictual equilibrium' involves a similar tension between the self-devised rhythmic conventions that characterize his verse and the traditional rhythms of classical metrical verse. Réda subverts, for example, the traditional requirement to pronounce all mute Es in poetry, but does so in a way that still depends on that tradition. We might even say that his poetry places greater value on the mute E than more conventional verse, because his use of the mute E varies situationally: the reader must attend to the placement of each mute E in order to determine its rhythmic value. Will it be pronounced or not? If so, how heavily should it be stressed? It is not possible simply to assume its value, as is often done in conventional metrical analyses. Réda's poetry demands a certain kind of attention to this variability, which he calls 'elasticity', and which entails 'using (thus also not using) the fixity of syllabic metre to obtain a sort of dynamic sur-regularity, which I have on occasion, perhaps somewhat recklessly, called swing' (88).

This dual refusal — of blind conformism to but also outright revolt against tradition — is central to Réda's view of his poetic mission. He sees himself as participating in a quest to reinvigorate the French language that involves bringing the conventions of poetic diction up to date, notably by opening them up to 'the cadence of spoken language' (73). The treatment of the mute E plays an important role in this reform, as only those Es 'that subsist *when one speaks*' are to be retained (73, emphasis in original). To illustrate his point, he explains how the overheard expression 'contre ce con de strapontin' is actually pronounced 'contre c'con d'strapontin', or even 'skondstrap' (83). We see here what Réda's poetic vocation shares with Raymond Queneau's proposed linguistic reforms, theorized in *Bâtons, chiffres et lettres* (*Bars, Numbers and Letters*) and illustrated in his novels.[11] But whereas Queneau draws on the resources of reformed spelling conventions to highlight the expressive power of colloquial speech, Réda most typically uses the constraints of metrical verse to draw out and explore its characteristic rhythmic values. It is, for example, this habit of eliding all possible syllables in spoken colloquial French that is at the origin of his invention of the 'vers mâché' (the 'chewed line', in which all expendable vowels are 'swallowed', as they are in colloquial speech).

Réda sees the resources of metrical verse (he shows little inclination for free verse) as an important tool in this quest because it makes explicit the framework against which he constructs his own rhythmic experiments. Poetry in this view is to be understood not as a Romantic expression of interiority but as a listening to the resources of the language itself. Thus poets — and this, for Réda, is the principal failing of most contemporary French poets — must learn to pay closer attention to the ways in which French is actually spoken: 'One is constantly troubled by such indifference to the laws and resources of the language in its reality. The French language is rhythmical. One would like to perceive objectively this rhythm, not subject oneself for no good reason to so-called "interior" tempos' (57). Subjective self-expression and the 'interiority' of the poet, then, are of only secondary interest here. What counts for Réda is an 'objective' exploration of 'the resources of the language in its reality'.

But how can this objectivist approach to poetic language be squared with the goal of externalizing 'the rhythmic essence of the self', alluded to earlier? Is this language-first conception of poetic invention compatible with the larger goal of subject formation? Paradoxically, it seems, true individuality is achieved through tight discipline, not absolute freedom; it entails not self expression freed from any external constraints, but, on the contrary, a conscientious, objective, *selfless* study of one's art and the resources it makes available to the artist. In 'L'appareil absolu' (The Ultimate Apparatus), an essay from *Celle qui vient*, Réda describes this search in terms of a recurrent poetic fantasy of his, which is to invent 'a physics of poetry', thanks to which 'the phenomena that we judge immaterial or imagined — like feelings, memories, gods, ideas — become measurable frequencies, perceptible waves' (25). The artist, then, is more of an explorer or scientific investigator than a creator in the demiurgic, Romantic sense of that term. The process of artistic creation involves constant research into the laws that govern our use of language, not the effusions of someone who can say anything he wants. This attitude toward artistic creation puts the concept of inspiration in an entirely different light. Inspiration, for Réda, is marked by a retrospective sense of inevitability, of necessity, of bringing to light some universal law that one had been obeying unwittingly up to that point.

Intuition, the sense that something is right because it feels right, plays an important role in this process, but marks only the first step. Intuition acts as the catalyst for the more systematic explorations to follow. Consider how Réda explains his lifelong devotion to verse written in 14-syllable lines. This is a quite unusual verse length in French but it is, he insists, the line that comes most naturally to him. He emphasizes on several occasions his instinctive, 'visceral' preference for the 14-syllable line, noting, for example, that even as a youth trying dutifully to write standard 12-syllable alexandrines, he usually found himself writing 14-syllable lines.[12]

It is here, perhaps, that Réda's theory of rhythm meets up most tellingly with the theory of the self evoked by Lacoue-Labarthe and Meschonnic. For Réda, his inability to escape from the 14-syllable line is an expression of the forces that made him who he is. This kind of spontaneous affinity is the mark of authentic individuality that he seeks in his writing: 'Thus in the poems that presumably I approve, since I published them, it is almost always [the spontaneity] of the metrical cadence [and] the spontaneity of the rhyme that convinced me of their probable validity' (94). He seeks to ground all of his poetic choices in determinants that impose themselves on him intuitively. Paradoxically, the poetic subject is most fully himself when he is obeying outside forces. This is a point that is made repeatedly throughout his career, as in 'Le pied furtif de l'hérétique' (The heretic's furtive foot), a prose poem that ends with an image of the poet as a string instrument plucked by his environment: 'I am now no more than the vibration of these fundamental strings, taut like hope, full like love' (*Les Ruines de Paris*, 14). Similarly, in 'L'intermittent' (from *Celle qui vient*) he echoes Rimbaud's response to the long tradition of divinely inspired creation by figuring himself as a vessel or instrument through which the outside world speaks: 'Let it be, at last, *the Exterior* that speaks in the deserted space that is me' (16). Réda, then, sees his task as a poet as a bringing together of outside and inside, self and other, subject and object, observer and environment, a fact that goes a long way toward explaining his life-long commitment to writing *flâneur* poetry, whose specificity is precisely in its attentive attunement to the environment, rather than its ability to impose the will of the poet onto the environment.

The rhythms of place consciousness in 'Le Borrégo'

How does this multi-variable interaction between poet, language and place manifest itself in Réda's poetry? It is a relatively straightforward matter to show this in his verse poetry. I have explored elsewhere some of the varied and nuanced kinds of 'swing' that Réda is able to introduce into his verse, particularly through his use of the 14-syllable line and the 'vers mâché'.[13] Here, however, space constraints prevent me from trying to do justice to the full range of Réda's rhythmic experiments, and so I will move immediately on to a more difficult, but also, in light of Meschonnic's work, more urgent question, which is to show how Réda's rhythmic proclivities manifest themselves in his prose, and how they create the kinds of *signifiance* that are for Meschonnic the hallmark of true poetic invention.

My example is taken from a recent prose text titled 'Le Borrégo' (The Borrégo), which presents itself as an evocation of a nondescript street in Paris's 20th arrondissement.[14] Although 'Le Borrégo' is a longish, fairly discursive piece of expository writing, it concludes with an extraordinarily dense outburst, a veritable prose poem that is in many ways the *product* or *outcome* of the preceding essay, as if the entire point of the essay was to prepare the reader for this one paragraph, that could, and perhaps should, be left to stand on its own merits:

'Qui suis-je, moi qui sur une longueur de plus de trois cents mètres, sans un seul commerce en dehors de ces magasins désaffectés, assure une jonction commode mais pas indispensable (on me voit presque toujours déserte) entre la rue du Télégraphe et la rue Haxo; moi qui porte un nom d'origine mexicaine' (c'est-à-dire 'campagne-du-Mexique', je m'en doutais); 'qui n'ai que dans ta mémoire, et de seconde main, d'incertains souvenirs de châteaux, de guinguettes, de massacres d'otages; qui n'ai que dans ton cerveau une voix, une conscience autonomes, un secret? Je ne suis qu'un trait dans la figure invisible de ta vie, qu'un des passages innombrables où elle t'attire pour que tu ne la trouves jamais'. (89)

('Who am I, I who over a distance of more than three hundred metres, without a single business, apart from these defunct shops, provide a useful but not indispensable (I'm almost always seen empty) junction between Telegraph Street and Haxo Street; I who bear a name of Mexican origin' (meaning — I knew it! — the Mexican campaign [of Napoleon III]); 'whose uncertain memories of castles, cafés, and hostage massacres exist only in your memory, who has only in your mind a voice, an autonomous consciousness, a secret? I'm no more than a line in the invisible figure of your life, one of the innumerable passages to which it draws you so that you'll never find it.')

It is the street who speaks here, addressing the poet. The point of this prosopopoeia is to evoke the profound complicity between the poetic consciousness and the street, which manifests itself as a kind of two-way communication that takes place in (and thanks to) the poem.

How might we go about doing a rhythmic analysis of this text? We could imagine trying an old-fashioned metrical analysis of the kind that seeks out unmarked verse/metrical units hidden within the prose. That analysis might begin by noting that this piece breaks down fairly naturally into units of six and eight syllables that can, with a few exceptions, and taking into account the variable way in which Réda treats mute Es, be grouped into 14-syllable verses (which is, as we recall, Réda's 'default' line length in verse). This kind of analysis is surprisingly easy to carry out on this text, although it does require making a few questionable decisions that might be considered 'forcing'. This hypothetical reading might look something like this:

'Qui suis-j(e), moi qui sur une longueur / de plus de trois cents mètres,	14	(8+6)
sans un seul commerce en dehors / d(e) ces magasins désaffectés,	16	(8+8)
assure un(e) jonction commode / mais pas indispensable	14	(8+6)
(on m(e) voit presque toujours déserte) / entre la rue du Télégraphe	16	(8+8)
et la rue Haxo; moi qui porte / un nom d'origin(e) mexicaine'	16	(8+8)
(c'est-à-dire 'campagne-du / Mexiqu(e)', / je m'en doutais);	12	(6+6)
'qui n'ai qu(e) dans ta mémoire, / et de second(e) main, d'incertains	14	(6+8)
souv(e)nirs de châteaux, de guinguettes, / de massacres d'otages;	14	(8+6)
qui n'ai qu(e) dans ton cerveau / un(e) voix, une conscience autonomes,	14	(6+8)
un secret? Je n(e) suis qu'un / trait dans la figure invisible	14	(6+8)
d(e) ta vie, qu'un des passages / innombrables où elle t'attire	14	(6+8)
pour que tu ne la trouv(es) (/) jamais'.	8	(6+2)

Eleven of these seventeen units adhere to the pattern of the 14-syllable line. And even the exceptions tend to fall into highly significant groupings of either 16 syllables (=two groups of 8, which might be considered a by-product of the role that 8-syllable units play in the 14-syllable line), or 8 syllables, as in the final unit, which acts as a clausula.

Given everything we've already discussed about Réda's instinctive preference for 14-syllable lines, and his self-confessed tendency to write prose that 'starts trotting along in verses of 14 feet' (*Celle qui vient*, 73), we might feel tempted to stop here, simply taking this text as proof of Réda's proclivity for groupings of 14-syllables and the extent of that unit's penetration into his poetic psyche. That, however, would be a mistake. As Benoît de Cornulier reminds us in 'Problèmes d'analyse rythmique du non-métrique' (Problems of rhythmic analysis of the non-metrical), the fact that there are no fixed rhythmic conventions in prose means that we must always beware of the temptation to force the issue, to bend the text's natural rhythms to fit our preconceived ideas.[15] Worse yet, this kind of analysis implicitly subordinates prose to verse, as if the aesthetic value of any prose text was determined by the extent to which it approximated verse. This, however, runs contrary to the spirit of both Réda and Meschonnic, whose respective theories of rhythm are explicitly founded on a belief that the value of any rhythmic profile derives from its origin in spontaneous, intuitive practices, not its conformity to metrical norms.

Given these reservations about the 'metrification' of prose texts, I would propose a different approach, one guided by Meschonnic's insistence on the organic interdependency of rhythm and meaning. Rather than using Meschonnic's somewhat unwieldy notational system, though, I will instead lay out this passage on the page in a way that highlights its logico-syntactical structure. The goal is to emphasize the ways in which the syllabic rhythms of the text interact dialectically with its semantic and syntactic structures, which enter in turn into large-scale rhythmic relations with each other. There is an overall semantic *intention* that shapes the macro-structures of the linguistic performance but that is in turn always overdetermined by the morphological constraints of the language and the series of more or less subconscious linguistic decisions made on the fly by the poet. These interactions shape each other in a complex process that works like a positive feedback loop.

Crucial to this analysis is the rhythmic role of the sub-clauses within the hierarchical semantic and syntactical structure of each sentence. My analysis represents this hierarchy by arraying the clauses from left to right, with the main clause furthest to the left, the first layer of subordinate clauses indented one level to the right, and so on.

'Qui suis-je,
     moi qui
               sur une longueur / de plus de trois cents mètres,
                  sans un seul commerce
                     en dehors de ces magasins désaffectés,
            assure une jonction / commode mais pas indispensable
                (on me voit presque toujours déserte)
            entre la rue du Télégraphe / et la rue Haxo;

moi qui

porte un nom d'origine mexicaine'
(c'est-à-dire 'campagne-du-Mexique',
je m'en doutais);

'qui

n'ai que dans ta mémoire,   [6]
et de seconde main,   [6]
d'incertains souvenirs   [6]
de châteaux, de guinguettes,   [6]
de massacres d'otages;   [6]

qui

n'ai que dans ton cerveau   [6]
une voix, une conscience autonomes, / un secret?

Je ne suis

qu'un trait dans la figure invisible de ta vie,
qu'un des passages innombrables
où elle t'attire pour que / tu ne la trouves / jamais.

The rhythmic vitality of this passage is clearly semantically driven: its numerous subordinate clauses are intertwined with the main clause in a way that forces readers to track each of these units individually while trying to hold them all in memory at the same time. After the fanfare of the opening main clause ('Qui suis-je, moi...?'), the rest of the sentence is, in a grammatical sense, unnecessary: it all boils down to this single, simple, (and quintessentially autobiographical) question: Who am I? Clearly though, what is important *rhythmically* in this sentence is not the main clause but the accumulation of sub-clauses. The repetitive nature of the 'moi qui... moi qui... qui... qui...' structure entails a sharp rise in intensity with each 'qui', in order to refocus attention on the main question ('who am I, I who...?') and also to distinguish this question from the layers of subordinate clauses, each of which must be read with a different level of intensity in order to keep them logically distinct from the main clause and from each other. Rhythmically speaking, then, it is the word 'qui' (repeated 5 times) that makes possible the great length of the first sentence by subdividing it into cognitively manageable units.

We might also notice the extended sub-clause introduced by the third 'qui', which features a list of 'uncertain memories' that has a suggestively mechanical rhythmic profile. The list-like quality of this passage is signalled rhythmically by the series of six-syllable clauses, which are clearly indicated semantically (as opposed to being an artificial, 'metrical' subdivision of the sentence). These groupings of six-syllable units also suggest that most conventional of units of French verse, the alexandrine. Whether premeditated or not, the effect of this rhythmic profile is to emphasize the semantic function of the sub-clause, which highlights in ironic fashion the fact that the all-but-forgotten material realities of the historical episode from which the street takes its name are lost for everyone except the poet, who himself has only vague 'second-hand' awareness of these realities (since they were acquired through research triggered by his curiosity about the name of the street).

The final point I would make about this passage is the disguised pa-rallelism between the second sentence and the first, which, with the help of a tightly ordered rhythmic progression, brings this passage (and the entire essay) to a satisfying close. This is a declarative sentence, and much shorter than the first, yet it echoes crucial rhythmic features of the preceding question, including the plosive [k] sounds (which become 'qu'un… qu'un… que…') and the limiting negation 'Je ne suis que', which is emphasized in both. Although this second sentence is much shorter and syntactically simpler than the first, it also thrives on the syntactic, rhythmic, and logical tension created by the stacking of subordinate clauses, which generates increasing amounts of pressure for closure, since the reader must stretch to retain all of this in memory while working out how each successive clause relates logically to what precedes.

We might also say that the relative brevity of this sentence, combined with its declarative mode, helps it to function effectively as a clausula. Indeed, the overall structure of the passage (long build-up, short resolution) is echoed within the final sentence: the sense of finality created by the last word, 'jamais', suggests the need for a dramatic pause before pronouncing the word, which has the effect of isolating it rhythmically. This final effect is prepared by an interesting tightening of the rhetorical screws carried out in this sentence through its rhythmic structure. After the introductory 'Je ne suis', the sentence lends itself to a reading that divides it into four successively smaller syllabic units (12, 8, 6, 4, and then, after a dramatic pause, the 2 syllables of jamais).

Needless to say, there is much else that could be said about the rhythmic profile of this passage. Let me instead close with two interpretive questions: First, why did Réda design this passage in this particularly dense, convoluted way? For the same reason, I think, that he decided to close his essay on the rue Borrégo with a prosopopoeia: to highlight the *interconnectedness* of all of the various elements in play in the relationship between the street, the poet, and his language. It is not any of the street's traits, singly or severally, that make up the unique identity of the street, but rather their confluence, in the consciousness of the poet, who has tried to render this confluence manifest by intertwining the various elements within the organic bonds of a single multilayered grammatico-rhythmic structure able to establish the kind of 'miraculous conflictual equilibrium' that is at the heart of Reda's definition of swing.

Finally, what, we might ask, does this piece have to tell us about the theory of rhythm? We have already seen hints of what a rhythmic analysis can *show* about the contribution of rhythm to the poem's meaning. But the last sentence suggests that this text could also be construed as a subtle commentary on the status of rhythm in prose poetry. Indeed, this street that is speaking to us is also a self-described 'passage' (un des passages innombrables), a term that could be applied to the text itself. If so, then the word 'innombrable' (innumerable) takes on an important secondary connotation, since, as a prose text, it remains, as we have seen, resistant to quantitative analysis — it is itself innumerable. It might tempt us into a quantitative analysis, much as the street draws us in ('elle t'attire pour que...'), but only to remind us that, if it is rhythm we're seeking, we'll never find it ('...pour que tu ne la trouves jamais').[16]

NOTES

1   Aviram mentions Julia Kristeva, Philippe Lacoue-Labarthe, Jacques Lacan, and Henri Meschonnic, presenting Charles Bernstein as an American fellow traveller. See Amittai Aviram, *Telling Rhythm* (Ann Arbor: University of Michigan Press, 1994) and 'The Meaning of Rhythm', in *Between Philosophy and Poetry: Writing, Rhythm, History*, edited by Massimo Verdicchio and Robert Burch (New York: Continuum, 2002), 161–70.

2   Philippe Lacoue-Labarthe, 'The Echo of the Subject', in *Typography* (Stanford: Stanford University Press, 1989), 139–207.

3   I have dealt more extensively with this aspect of music in Lacoue-Labarthe's thought in 'Musical Imprints and Mimetic Echoes in Philippe Lacoue-Labarthe', *L'Esprit créateur*, 47:2 (Summer 2007), 17–32. For another perspective on Lacoue-Labarthe, see the two Aviram texts referenced above.

4   Even something as apparently obvious as the relationship between rhythm in poetry and in music can lead to misunderstandings. Aviram's study of rhythm is admirable in many respects, but he errs considerably in trying to force a musical, beat centered, definition of rhythm onto poetic discourse, as if the

recitation of verse could be regulated by a metronome. (See Aviram 2002, 163 and passim.)

5 Henri Meschonnic, *Critique du rythme* (Lagrasse: Verdier, 1982).

6 See Meschonnic, 71. See also David Evans's contribution to this volume, and Simon Jarvis's 'Musical Thinking: Hegel and the Phenomenology of Prosody', *Paragraph* 28 : 2 (July 2005), 57–71. Gabriella Bedetti's 'Henri Meschonnic: Rhythm As Pure Historicity', *New Literary History* 23 (1992), 431–50, gives a useful, concise, English-language introduction to the work of Meschonnic emphasizing its political aspirations. Her interview with Meschonnic, published in *Diacritics* (Fall 1988), 93–111, provides another excellent point of entry into Meschonnic's work, including a relatively straightforward definition of the term *signifiance*, which is central to his theory of rhythm.

7 See 'Problèmes d'analyse rythmique du non-métrique' (*Semen* 16, URL : http://semen.revues.org/document2736.html. Consulted 5 August 2008).

8 Jacques Réda, *L'Improviste* (Paris: Jallimard, 1990); *Anthologie des musiciens de jazz* (Paris: Stock, 1981).

9 By contrast, Réda associates conventional verse poetry with the mechanical clackety-clack of train travel. In 'Steamin' with Duke', from *L'Herbe des talus* (Paris: Gallimard, 1995), he writes of 'the rails of the alexandrine' and in *Celle qui vient à pas légers* (see below note 10) he remarks that 'metre introduces movement into rhythm in the same way that the tracks and their cross ties create that of the train. That is perhaps why the train has such powerful poetic virtues' (85).

10 Jacques Réda, *Celle qui vient à pas légers* (Montpellier: Fata Morgana, 1999). All translations from texts by Réda are my own.

11 *Zazie dans le métro* (Paris: Gallimard, 1959) begins, famously, with the word/ phrase *Doukipudonktan*, later resolved (more or less) as 'D'où qu'ils puent donc tant'. How to translate this? Perhaps: *Swydaystinklikdat*. Further evidence of Queneau's untranslatability can be seen in the fact that an English translation of *Bâtons, chiffres et lettres* (Paris: Gallimard, 1965) was published under the title *Numbers, Letters, Forms* (Champaign, IL: University of Illinois Press, 2007).

12 In *Celle qui vient*, he makes this point several times: 'A variety of unfathomable reasons have resulted in a certain fixation on my part on the 14-syllable line' (67). 'I have discovered that it is best (…) to write (…) in groups of sequences or measures that conform to the needs of my nervous system, which stamps its *feet* [pun intended] to demand reiteration of the 14' (72).

13 See my '*Paris à l'improviste*: Jacques Réda, Jazz, and Sub-Urban Beauty', *SubStance* 38 : 2 (2009), 89–112.

14 Jacques Réda, 'Le Borrégo,' in *Le vingtième me fatigue* (Paris: La Dogona, 2004).

15 Unpaginated web document. See footnote 7 for full reference.

16 I thank David Evans for this insight.

Leonid Martynov, Boris Slutsky and the Politics of Rhythm

Barry P. Scherr

Abstract:
Leonid Martynov (1905–80) and Boris Slutsky (1919–86) began to write during Stalin's reign and were aware of the contemporary official pressure to make literature more broadly accessible as well as of the highly experimental, and thus more difficult, poetry that had come into vogue during the years leading up to the Bolshevik revolution. Martynov's response was to create verse marked by ambiguity; he employs the graphic layout and internal rhyme to avoid predictability and easy interpretation, especially in a poem's opening lines. Slutsky, in contrast, often lacks the sense of rhythmic order that usually emerges in Martynov's poems. He may disrupt the rhythm unexpectedly or vary it so frequently that no overarching pattern appears. Both, whether by unsettling the rhythm or complicating its perception, manage to recall the freer and more experimental artistic milieu of the early twentieth century.

Keywords: rhythm, metre, poetry, Russian, Martynov, Slutsky, graphic layout, internal rhyme

> ... the Party was *against* rhythm, since rhythm excited
> the passions and was therefore anti-rational,
> and, by extension, anti Marxist.
>
> Josef Škvorecký, *The Miracle Game*

During the Soviet period Russian writers came to learn that the very structure of a literary work could become an issue of political import. By the mid-1920s the impetus for radical innovation in poetry and in prose — a hallmark of the Modernist movements in Russia since the 1890s — was coming up against the desire of the new regime to impose strictures not just on the content of literary works but also on their form. The Bolshevik leaders saw artists' endeavors as important and as capable of influencing and directing the broader public. A positive corollary of this belief was the government's providing significantly more support to the creative arts than was often the case elsewhere. Less positive was the attempt to limit or direct the kinds of art

Paragraph 33:2 (2010) 246–259
DOI: 10.3366/E0264833410000878

that was produced. In addition to putting constraints on the content, literary officials also wanted art to appeal generally to the masses and be broadly accessible. This goal militated against thematic complexity or obscurity as well as against the more experimental poetic forms.

The consequences of this policy held special significance for what might be termed the middle generation of 20th-century Russian poets. Most of the famous writers who emerged during the height of Modernism and prior to the Bolshevik upheaval — Anna Akhmatova, Boris Pasternak, Osip Mandelshtam, and Vladimir Mayakovsky, to list some of the best-known figures — were born between the 1880s and early 1890s. The youngest generation was born from the early 1930s on and came of age after the Second World War: Evgeny Evtushenko, Andrei Voznesensky, Bella Akhmadulina, and Joseph Brodsky, among others. Those who fall in the forty-year gap between these generations entered literature during the period of the most stringent controls on the arts; they have received relatively little attention in the West and for that matter have not always been fully acknowledged in Russia itself. The focus here is on two such writers: Leonid Martynov (1905–80), a native of Siberia who came of age early enough to be attracted to the Futurist movement (the same school that could claim Pasternak and Mayakovsky as adherents), and Boris Slutsky (1919–86), who, like Martynov, had a troubled relationship with literary officialdom in the Soviet Union and was highly influential on his younger contemporaries.

Russian verse had come to its maturity during roughly the second through the fourth decades of the nineteenth century, the time of Pushkin and his contemporaries. For virtually the whole of the century poetry was distinguished by a high degree of regularity in terms of both metre and rhyme, with poets overwhelmingly employing the familiar syllabo-tonic metres, most frequently iambs. Russian syllabo-tonic verse adheres to several strict rules. For instance, the final strong position in a verse line carries an obligatory stress, and stressing on the weak positions is limited to monosyllabic words in the disyllabic metres (iambs and trochees) and to mono- or disyllabic words in trisyllabic. The relatively long length of Russian words (about 2.7 syllables, on average) dictates that not all the strong positions in iambic and trochaic verse will be stressed. This feature, combined with the obligatory stress on the final strong position, helps create specific rhythmic patterns for Russian disyllabic metres. In all, they exhibit a greater degree of regularity and predictability than is typical of

English.[1] Furthermore, up to very recent times, Russian verse has been predominantly rhymed.

Significant changes took part around the turn of the twentieth century. Russian poets did not so much challenge the notion of rhythm per se, but they came to use less regular and less predictable forms alongside syllabo-tonic verse. The *dolnik*, in which the intervals between strong positions could be either one or two syllables, soon became widespread and for some emerged as the favored metre. Poets experimented broadly with a variety of accentual verse forms, and a handful began to write free verse. Innovative writers mixed syllabo-tonic metres in ways that were not permissible earlier or created new rhythms for even the established metres — rhythms that often did not follow the natural proclivities of the language.[2] Some of the Russian Futurists were especially radical in their approach to form, composing works in which pure sound, rather than meaning, provided the essence of the work or creating pictorial layouts of words on the page — experiments not dissimilar to the Dadaist works described by David Gascoigne in his article for this issue.

All of this came to a virtual halt with the official disapproval of highly experimental art. While free verse was enjoying ever-wider use in many other literary traditions, it nearly disappeared from Russian poetry, reemerging only during the 1950s and becoming a form used relatively widely only toward the end of the twentieth century. When poets did break away from syllabo-tonic poetry during the remainder of the Soviet period, they preferred the *dolnik*, which is still relatively regularized. In the epigraph to this paper the Czech émigré Josef Škvorecký was referring to music, but his point applies to poetry as well: just as the complex rhythms of jazz were seen to embody a threat to the order imposed by the state, so too were unusual rhythms in poetry regarded as something that might cause its audience to question other aspects of their regular (and regularized) existence.

Indeed, it is instructive to look at the very concept of rhythm as it came to be discussed by scholars. The Russian Formalist critics, who focused on texts and language rather than ideology, tended to view rhythm as a feature that imposes a kind of order on a text but is external to language. Thus Viktor Zhirmunsky, in a book originally published in 1925, described rhythm as 'the actual sequence of strong and weak sounds, which arise as a result of the interaction between the natural qualities of the linguistic material and metrical rules'.[3] Boris Tomashevsky, building upon some of the concepts in Zhirmunsky's book, noted further that the 'rhythmic impulse regulates not only phenomena that (...) are objectivized in traditional metrics, but an entire set of dimly perceived but undoubtedly aesthetically efficacious aspects of verse speech'.[4] Both, in other words, regard rhythm as something that, while different from language, reacts with it and other phenomena to help create the effect of verse. However, Leonid Timofeev, whose extensive writings about verse bore the imprint of the Party's views on aesthetic matters, in one of his late works claimed that it was incorrect to see verse as rhythmic speech; rather, it is a 'system of word combinations, which creates a meaningful and aesthetically significant content, with its expressiveness based on the repetition of rhythmic sound components of language'.[5] The differences are subtle but critical. For Timofeev, unlike the Formalists, rhythm is a part of language, rather than an extralinguistic element that acts upon it. Timofeev is ultimately interested primarily in meaning, in the message that words convey, and is suspicious of placing too much emphasis on those factors that do not have a clear semantic import.

During the Soviet era the metrical and rhythmical experiments introduced around the turn of the twentieth century did not so much go away as remain in the background, cultivated by a handful of poets such as Martynov and Slutsky. Despite reservations sometimes expressed by the more Party-line critics, they managed to call attention to the role of rhythm, which they perceived as functioning alongside but separate from language, in conveying the sense of a poem. Some of their ability to go against the tendencies of mainstream Soviet writing stemmed from the declaration, made by Stalin himself, that Mayakovsky, a highly experimental writer in his day, was a great 'Soviet' poet — this despite the likelihood that his 1930 suicide in part resulted from the growing conflict between his free-wheeling artistic sensibility and the social order he had once celebrated. The official acceptance of Mayakovsky created an opening for those who came to the fore during the decades following his death to employ rhythmically innovative verse. Thus in an article from the 1960s describing Mayakovsky's influence on poets writing after World War II, E. V. Ermilova cites with approval both Martynov and, especially, Slutsky as poets who absorbed various lessons from Mayakovsky, including those that involved breaking away from the rhythmic norms of the nineteenth century.[6]

While both Martynov and Slutsky provided important links back to the earlier period and significantly influenced their younger contemporaries, their approaches to matters of rhythm differed in interesting ways. Martynov was interested in borders and in borderline states, frequently writing, for example, about the boundary between the natural and the man-made worlds. Perhaps not surprisingly for a person who did a fair amount of translating, he also explored the margins between one means of expression and another. As a sometime writer of non-fiction, he also had a special interest in the differences between poetry and prose. A handful of his works are written out in paragraphs but contain rhyme and metre, and in several poems he ruminated on the shift from one medium to the other.

Martynov's originality appears in his techniques for complicating the perception of a work's basic structural form. In Russian syllabo-tonic verse the metre is generally clear after a single line, or in any case after several. Indeed, a basic principle of the tradition is predictability, in regard to both metre and rhyme. Martynov, in contrast, frequently writes poems that are unpredictable, particularly in the opening lines, where it can be difficult to discern either the metre or the rhythm[7]:

	Слова!	wS
	Сова	wS
	И та способна вымолвить:	wS wS wS ws
	«Угу!»	wS
5	В рычанье льва	wS wS
	Услышать можно голос естества.	wS wS wS ws wS
	У каждого	wS ws
	свои права	wS wS
	В своем кругу —	wS wS
10	И у кузнечика и у кита.	ws wS ws ws wS
	И только я	wS wS
	Ни слова не могу	wS ws wS
	Сказать порой, замкнув себе уста,	wS wS wS wS wS
	Совсем как лютому врагу,	wS wS ws wS
15	Как будто только молча я не лгу.[8]	wS wS wS wS wS[9]

(Words! / Even an owl / can utter: / — 'Ooo hoo!' // In the lion's growl / You can hear nature's voice. // All have / Their rights / In their own circle — / Both the grasshopper and the whale. // And only I / At times can't say / A single word, my lips are sealed, / Just like before a fierce enemy / As if I don't lie only when silent.)

At the beginning of this 1970 work, and at intervals elsewhere in the poem, Martynov creates a 'column': the verse line is broken up into segments, and then each segment is placed underneath the other. The borders between verse lines then are most typically determined by the rhyme scheme. This type of graphic layout began to appear in Russian poetry early in the twentieth century and was popularized by Mayakovsky, who likely inspired Martynov in this instance.[10] Martynov makes this form especially challenging by frequently employing internal rhyme, so that it becomes difficult to perceive the verse structure at the start; only toward the end of this excerpt is it clear that the most frequent line type in the poem is an underlying iambic pentameter. Note that the first two lines seem to rhyme (Slová / Sová), possibly creating lines with just one-foot iambs. However, a consideration of the first half dozen lines together suggests that the first four rhyme words are Sová / Ugú! [rhyming with krugú in line 9]/ l'vá / estestvá, creating four verse lines that are in alternating iambic dimeter and pentameter. But this structure is resolved only upon a second or third reading; the combination of internal rhyme and the poem's layout on the page complicates perception of the poem's rhythm.[11]

The next four lines (7–10) are even more complicated. If 'prava' (which would rhyme with three of the four previous rhyme words) is meant to mark the boundary of a metrical line, then the four lines combine into three: an iambic tetrameter (lines 7–8), followed by a dimeter and pentameter. However, the strong enjambement at the border of line 8 and 9 hints that lines 7–9 on the page might comprise a single hexameter line. Both readings are possible, and so the fifteen lines on the page may contain either 10 or 11 metrical lines, depending on the readers' interpretation, leaving the poem's structure uncertain.

The metrical ambiguity suggests a certain unease about allowing for determinacy, a sense that is in keeping with the content. Briefly summarized, this segment is saying that animals can make utterances, but that the poet is afraid to say a single word for fear of lying. While the message changes toward the poem's end (which I have not quoted), in this passage Martynov echoes a famous Russian poem (Fedor Tiutchev's 1830s 'Silentium!', with the line 'An uttered thought is a lie' (Mysl' izrechennaia est' lozh')). The indeterminate rhythm, which slows any effort to read the poem, makes it seem that the phrases and lines are being put down with difficulty or reluctance, as if the poet frets that even articulating his notion could lead to a falsehood.

If the posthumously published work given below appears at first to be relatively straightforward in its rhythmic qualities, the complex sound patterns quickly suggest that much is going on beneath the surface:[12]

Кто	W
Сроду	S w
Сочинял за одой оду,	s wS wS wSw
Кто годы погружался в переводы,	WS ws wS ws wSw
5 Кто замыкался в эпос, точно в крепость,	Ws wS wS wS wSw
А кто срывался в прозу, будто в пропасть!	wS wS wS wS wSw
Но с более обрывистого брега	wS ws wS ws wSw
Я без оглядки со всего разбега	ws wS ws wS wSw
Всегда кидался в лирику, как в реку,	wS wS wS ws wSw
10 И плыл, и плыл по этому потоку,	wS wS wS ws wSw
Как будто с грустью уносимый к устью,	wS wS ws wS wSw
А все–таки добрался до истока,	wS ws wS ws wSw
Наперекор плывя —	ws wS wS
Навстречу Веку!	wS wS

(Martynov, 519)

(Some / Since birth / Have composed ode after ode, / Some have been immersed in translating for years, / Some have been locked inside the epos, as though in a fortress, / And some have fallen into prose, as though into an abyss! / But from a steeper shore / Without glancing back I always rushed / At full tilt into lyrics, as into a river, / And I swam and swam in this stream, / Seemingly being carried away with sadness to its mouth / And nonetheless I reached the source, / Swimming against the current — / To meet my epoch!)

The poem implies that switching to prose would lead to oblivion. For that matter, not much promise is held for those who become immersed in some of the grander poetic forms or who occupy themselves solely with translation. The true challenge is lyric verse, and this endeavor involves both risk (the leap into the river) and difficulty; however, by overcoming resistance and going in a direction of one's own it is possible to arrive at an understanding of the age. In this regard the poem seems almost a direct response to the fear of utterance in 'Words'.

The work is in iambic pentameter, though the metre at the beginning is again less clear, with the first iambic pentameter line divided into three lines on the page and internal rhyme allowing for an ambiguous reading (the second line on the page rhymes with the third). What is distinct about this poem is the manner in which the internal rhyme continues throughout, making it difficult for the reader (and even more so for the listener) to distinguish the borders of the pentameter lines. Thus in the fourth line 'gódy' not only rhymes with 'perevódy' at the end of the line, but, approximately, with 'Sródu' in the second. Thus it is possible to read the lines as 'Kto Sródu / Sochiniál za ódoi ódu, / Kto gódy / pogruzhálsia v perevódy', with the two verse lines divided into four. Lines 5–6 present an even more complicated picture, where the rhyme between the word at the comma and that at the end is stronger than the end rhyme: consider 'épos / krépost'' and 'prózu / própast'', as opposed to the end rhyme 'krépost' / própast'', where the stressed vowels differ even if the consonants after those vowels are the same. Also, 'zamykálsia' and 'sryválsia' form yet another internal rhyme, so that there are two different ways in which the two lines could be read as four, or they could even be read as six, rhyming ABBACC (zamykálsia /épos / krépost''/ sryválsia / prózu / própast'). The challenging aspects of this poem do not end there. For instance, 'réku' (line 9) does not find its rhyme pair until the last line of the poem ('Véku'), while line eleven is essentially unrhymed, though it contains a strong internal rhyme: 'grúst'iu / úst'iu'. This use of an occasional unrhymed line of course further complicates the perception of a poem's structure and is a technique Martynov may well have borrowed from Mayakovsky.[13] By employing rhyme in unpredictable ways that disrupt the recognition of the metre and thus a sense of the rhythm, he 'delyricizes' the lyric poetry which he advocates, weakening the perceptibility of the line structure even as he turns to one of the most familiar Russian metrical forms. The poem is ultimately about challenges, about leaping into the unknown. The disjuncture between the easily recognizable iambic pentameter and the challenging graphic layout dislodges readers from the customary and places them in unfamiliar territory.

Boris Slutsky, half a generation younger than Martynov, first started to publish poetry during World War II, in which he served at the front, and the war appears as a central theme in much of his work, particularly that written earlier on. Like Martynov, he gained renown as a poet only gradually. His first post-war publication did not appear until 1953, and his first collection came out only in 1957, when he was already in his late thirties. Part of the issue for Slutsky was his willingness to address topics that were on the edge of what was acceptable to the Soviet regime and sometimes over the edge. A few works expressing an ironical atittude toward Stalin were published during the anti-Stalin campaign of the early 1960s but then did not appear in print again until several years after Slutsky's death, well into the period of glasnost. Other poems, including many dealing with anti-Semitism, were essentially written only 'for the [desk] drawer', to use the phrase common among Russian writers, and were not publishable at all during his lifetime.

Sometimes Slutsky seems to grant poetry an almost mystical power. Thus in 'Upon the very day the war concluded. . .' he observes that significant events turn out to express themselves through verse:

В тот день, когда окончилась война,	wS wS wS ws wS
вдруг оказалось: эта строчка — ямбы, —	Ws wS wS wS wSw
хоть никогда не догадался я бы,	ws wS ws wS wSw
что будет метр стиха иметь она.	wS wS wS wS wS
Я полагал: метр вздоха и метр крика.	ws wS WS ws WSw
Я думал: метр обвала тишины, —	wS wS wS ws wS
но оказалось — строчками должны,	ws wS wS ws wS
стихами становиться эти звуки.[14]	wS ws wS wS wSw

> (Upon the very day the war concluded. . . / it suddenly turned out that this line is iambic/ though I never would have guessed / that it would have the metre of verse. // I supposed: the metre of a sigh and the metre of a shout / I thought: the metre of an avalanche of silence, —/but it turned out these sounds ought to become lines,/ become verses.)

He begins with a strikingly prosaic statement, and then seems startled to realize that the line is in iambic verse.[15] He had expected the end of the war to take on other rhythms — of a sigh, a shout, or even silence — but instead the rhythm of poetry turns out to be most suited to express the sense of the event. As Slutsky ruminates on those other rhythms, in the first line of the second stanza, he twice places the strongly stressed Russian word 'metr' in a weak position; that, along with the absence of a stress on the fourth strong position (coinciding with the word 'i', meaning 'and') essentially breaks the iambic rhythm: three unstressed syllables at the beginning of the line are followed by three that are strongly stressed (a verb and two nouns); the next two are unstressed and the subsequent two stressed. Using x and X for unstressed and stressed syllables, the schema of the line is as follows xxxXXXxxXXx. Without the context of its surroundings, it would be hard to regard this sequence as iambic. The line thus rhythmically as well as semantically suggests that various kinds of rhythm may exist in the world; rhythm comes to convey a self-referential message.

Slutsky's use of metre and rhythm is in some ways deceptive. On the one hand, like 'Upon the very day the war concluded...', he often remains completely within the syllabo-tonic tradition, albeit even in these instances he is capable of inserting a line that breaks with the dominant rhythm of the poem. On the other, he can write poems where the rhythm is sufficiently irregular that he comes close to writing free verse.[16] If Martynov complicates the beginnings of many poems by making the form difficult to perceive or outright ambiguous but then often glides into an underlying and almost reassuring rhythm, Slutsky prefers not to let his poems settle down: he interrupts the established rhythm in unpredictable ways and in extreme cases switches metres almost at will. For much of his more rhythmically experimental verse, as in the work below, poetry itself serves as either the main or a subsidiary subject, whether he is writing about its inherent qualities, how it is made, or its significance.

Целый народ предпочел стихи	XxxXxxXxX
для выражения не только чувств —	xxxXxxxXxX
мыслей. Чем же это кончится?	XxXxXxXxx
Стих — не ходьба. Поэзия — пляска.	XxxXxXxxXx
Целый народ под ритмы лязга	XxxXxXxXx
национальных инструментов	xxxXxxxXx
в народных оркестрах	xXxxXx
не ходит, а пляшет.	xXxxXx
Чем же это кончится?	XxXxXxx

(Slutsky, III: 141)

(The entire nation preferred verses / for expressing not only feelings — / but also thoughts. Where will it end? / Verse is not walking. Poetry is dance. / The entire nation to the rhythms of the clanging / of national instruments / in folk orchestras / does not walk but dances. / Where will it end?)

Interestingly, as several other articles in this issue illustrate, many of the literary works concerned with rhythm have music as a major theme. Here, the rhythm changes with such frequency and in places is so irregular that the graphic layout is crucial for perceiving the work as poetry. The first line employs a four-stress *dolnik*, while the second, like the opening of 'Upon the very day the war concluded...' offers a rather prosaic statement that just happens to be in iambic pentameter. This shift in metre, the absence of rhyme and the strong enjambement between lines 1 and 2, as well as between 2 and 3, combine to not allow the reader to perceive the opening as rhythmic, even as the layout on the page declares the author's intent that the lines are part of a poem. In contrast, the Russian phrase for 'of national instruments' (line 6) turns out to form another seemingly prosaic line, but one that actually consists of iambs, while the two following lines are both in amphibrachic dimeter, creating the feel of dance that is a topic of the poem. In addition, the third line contains trochaic tetrameter and the last trochaic trimeter. Slutsky destroys any possibility of knowing what the next line might bring; yet by employing two lines each of trochees, iambs and amphibrachs, he does allow a sense of rhythm into the poem, however variable.

More often, Slutsky simply employs regular metres in ways that go against the norms of the Russian poetic tradition. Nila Friedberg has described Slutsky as a 'rule-breaker': whereas Joseph Brodsky, a 'rule-maker', disrupted the rhythm in some of his iambic lines in ways that suggest he had formulated a set of principles for doing so, Slutsky simply defied the laws regulating Russian iambic verse, not creating any predictability in the ways he would interrupt the iambic rhythm.[17] See, for instance, line 8 in the following poem:

Я думаю, что следует начать	wS ws wS ws wS
С начала.	wS w
Не с конца. Не с середины.	s wS ws wSw
Не с последствий,	sw Sw
а с первопричины,	sw sw Sw
4 Рассвету место дать, а не ночам.	wS wS wS ws wS
Я был мальчишкою с душою вещей,	wS wS ws wS wSw
Каких в любой поэзии не счесть.	wS wS wS ws wS
Своею частью и своею честью,	wS wS ws wS wSw
8 Считающим эту часть и честь.	wS ws [ ]S wS wS

       (Slutsky, I: 60–61)

(I think that one should begin / From the beginning \ Not from the end, Not from the middle. / Not from consequences, \ but from the first cause/ One should favor the dawn, and not the nights. // I was just a little boy with a prophetic soul, / Of the sort that are innumerable in any [national] poetry. / Who considered this fate and honor / To be his own fate and honor.)

The quotation consists of the poem's first two stanzas, or 8 of the 48 lines. In the first stanza Slutsky uses a 'stepladder' layout. Like columns, this graphic device was popularized by Mayakovsky and involves breaking up the verse line by indenting one or more segments. Note that whereas placing each segment directly underneath another in a column can make it difficult to perceive the boundaries of the verse line, with a stepladder layout line boundaries remain readily discernible even as individual words or phrases receive heightened prominence.

In this seemingly autobiographical work Slutsky describes his early poetry, when he was similar to everyone else and his thinking was locked into plain iambs. The poem's rhythm, though, tells a different and more complex story. If the poem is written mainly in iambic pentameter, line 3 is trochaic. The appearance of trochaic lines in an essentially iambic poem was virtually unknown in Russian before the twentieth century and likely reflects another instance of Mayakovsky's influence.[18] The rhythm is again disrupted in line 8, with its two-syllable interval between the strong positions; the line seems to be missing a weak syllable. The poem's rhythm foreshadows its chief theme, which is about gaining freedom from imposed forms and allowing poetry to finds its own voice and its own rhythm.

What, finally, do these examples tell us about the attitudes of Martynov and Slutsky toward rhythm? We see that for both, even as they break with nineteenth-century conventions, rhythm retains its importance for establishing the expectation against which they create their works. However, rhythm is not simply subsidiary to semantics, as Timofeev would have it, but, more along the lines suggested by Zhirmunsky and Tomashevsky, takes on independent significance in organizing verse. Writing at a time when the state-controlled literary establishment advocated works that were straightforward in terms of both their content and their form, the two poets composed poetry that defied easy definition in both regards. Martynov reveals a knack for creating poems that thrive on ambiguity; he does not so much break with the rhythmic norms of Russian verse as write lines that call out to be read in a variety of ways at once. If these works may ultimately settle into a recognizable verse form, he avoids predictability and easy interpretation, especially in a poem's beginning lines. Slutsky often lacks the sense of a rhythmic order that nearly always emerges in Martynov's poetry. He finds that rhythmic verse has surprising power ('Upon the very day the war concluded...') but also, as in this last poem, considers regularity of form at times confining. He may disrupt the rhythm at odd moments or create a work in which the identifiable rhythms vary so frequently that it is difficult to define an overarching pattern. Of the two, his work turns out to be the more discordant in its rhythmic disruptions as well as darker in its content. For both, though, the underlying expectation of rhythm is crucial, embodying the tradition within which and often against which they compose their verse. By disrupting the rhythm or complicating its perception they both challenged their readers and evoked the spirit of experimentation that had flourished in Russian poetry at the turn of the twentieth century.

NOTES

1   The scholar Kiril Taranovsky discovered two 'laws' that determined the basic rhythmic tendencies for Russian iambs and trochees: a clear propensity to stress the first strong position that follows the first weak position in the line, and an alternation of more and less frequently stressed strong positions. This second tendency operates most powerfully at the end of the line (with the constant stress on the final strong position) and then moves backwards through the line in a wave-like fashion. Taranovsky provided a concise summary of his many years' research in 'O ritmicheskoi strukture russkikh dvuslozhnykh razmerov,' in *Poetika i stilistika russkoi literatury*, edited by M. P. Alekseev (Leningrad: Nauka, 1971), 420–9.

2   And thus did not conform to the laws put forth by Taranovsky. For concise descriptions of developments both during the period of Russian Modernism and for the entire Soviet epoch, see Chapters Five and Six of M. L. Gasparov, *Ocherk istorii russkogo stikha: Metrika, ritmika, rifma, strofika*, 2nd (enlarged) edition (Moscow: Fortuna Limited, 2000).

3   V. Zhirmunskii, *Vvedenie v metriku: Teoriia stikha*, reprinted in his *Teoriia stikha* (Leningrad: Sovetskii pisatel', 1975), 16. Translations of both prose and poetry passages in this essay are my own; in translating the verse I sacrifice elegance in order to more closely follow the syntax and word order of the Russian.

4   B. V. Tomashevskii, *O stikhe* (Leningrad: Priboi, 1929), 58–9.

5   Leonid Timofeev, *Slovo v stikhe* (Moscow: Sovetskii pisatel', 1982), 140.

6   E. V. Ermilova, 'Maiakovskii i sovremennyi russkii stikh' in *Maiakovskii i sovetskaia literatura: Stat'i, publikatsii, materialy i soobshcheniia*, edited by Z. S Papernyi (Moscow: Nauka, 1964), 231–56.

7   For a general treatment of Martynov's strategies, including a lengthier discussion of 'Slova', see my 'Nachinaia s nachala: Zametki o stikhoslozhenii Leonida Martynova', in *Slavianskii stikh VII: Lingvistika i struktura stikha*, edited by M. L. Gasparov and T. V. Skulacheva (Moscow: Iazyki slavianskoi kul'tury, 2004), 137–46.

8   Leonid Martynov, *Stikhotvoreniia i poemy*, compiled by N. K. Starshinov (Moscow: Sovremennik, 1985), 378.

9   I follow convention here in showing the rhythmic pattern of syllabo-tonic poetry by using 'w' for the weak positions, syllables that the meter predicts will be unstressed, while 's' designates strong positions, or ictuses, that the abstract metrical pattern indicates as carrying stress. A lower-case letter means that the specific syllable is unstressed, an upper-case letter that it is stressed. For most non-syllabo-tonic verse it is impossible to speak of strong or weak positions, and therefore I use 'x' to designate an unstressed syllable and 'X' for a stressed syllable.

10 For a good overview of both this technique and the so-called 'stepladder' form (discussed below in connexion with Slutsky), see Herbert Eagle, 'The Semantic Influence of Step-Ladder and Column Forms in the Poetry of Belyj, Majakovskij, Voznesenskij, and Roždestvesnkij', *Forum at Iowa on Russian Literature* I (1976), 1–19.

11 S. V. Savchenko, who wrote several articles on Martynov's verse, has described the phenomenon as the 'principle of the indeterminate beginning', in which the opening line(s) do not, on their own, allow the reader to predict the work's underlying meter. See his 'Perekhodnye metricheskie formy v lirike Leonida Martynova (ot klassicheskikh metrov k neodnorodnomu stikhu)', in *Problemy preemstvennosti v literaturnom protsesse*, edited by Kh. A. Adibaev (Alma-Ata: Kazakhskii pedagogicheskii institut, 1985), 56–7.

12 For a detailed analysis of this work, see A. L. Zhovtis, 'Stikh Leonida Martynova v kontekste russkoi stikhotvornoi kul'tury', in *Khudozhestvennaia individual'nost' pisatelia i literaturnyi protsess (tvorchestvo L. Martynova)*, edited by E. G. Shik (Omsk: Omskii gosudarstvennyi pedagogicheskii institut, 1989), 26–8.

13 See Ermilova, 255.

14 Boris Slutskii, *Sobranie sochinenii v trekh tomakh* (Moscow: Khudozhestvennaia literatura, 1991), III, 123.

15 For remarks on the prosaic qualities of his verse see P. Lazarev, 'Kogda proza stanovitsia poeziei. . .', *Voprosy literatury* 11 : 1 (1967), 58–72.

16 See the introduction by G. S. Smith (who is also the editor and translator of the volume) to Boris Slutsky, *Things that Happened* (Moscow: GLAS Publishers; Chicago: Ivan R. Dee, distributor, 1999), 19–20.

17 Nila Friedberg, 'Rule-Makers and Rule-Breakers: Josesph Brodsky and Boris Slutsky as Reformers of Russian Rhythm', *The Russian Review* 68 : 4 (2009), 641–61. I am grateful to Professor Friedberg for providing her paper prior to its publication and for sharing some of her observations about Slutsky's versification.

18 Ermilova, 249.

Sacred Rhythms, Tired Rhythms: Dino Campana's Poetry

HELEN ABBOTT

Abstract:

Early twentieth-century Italian poetry experiences a crisis in confidence concerning the expressibility of rhythm. Dino Campana's writings exemplify the processes the poet goes through in order to write (about) rhythm. Rhythm is difficult to deal with because it is both sacred and tired. These two incarnations of rhythm lead Campana to different modes of expression; from more traditional definitions (in terms of metre or pulse) through to more fluid definitions (in terms of poetic form, syntax and metaphor). Two strands of analysis reveal themselves as central to understanding Campana's theoretical stance, namely fluidity and movement. These point to a careful veiling of rhythm which opens up new spaces for the articulation of something that, whilst difficult, remains the essence of poetry.

Keywords: Campana, rhythm, metre, Italian poetry, fluidity, movement, sacred rhythm, tired rhythm

In the writings of early twentieth-century Italian poets, there is an acknowledgement that rhythm is difficult. It is difficult to pin down what rhythm is and what it does; it is difficult to translate experiences of rhythm (from nature, from music, from everyday life); and it is difficult to write (about) rhythm. That difficulty stems partly from a dual perception of rhythm, as both a source of poetry, and a threat to it. There is something sacred about rhythm, something mysterious which remains out of reach and cannot be explained, to the extent almost that rhythm cannot even be named, and yet seems to remain an essential element of the poetic. But rhythm can also appear as something tired and worn out, which needs to be exposed in order for poets not to succumb to its temptations. Poets' attempts to negotiate the relationship between these two manifestations of rhythm reveal a crisis of confidence concerning the expressibility of rhythm. This crisis, though it does not become the focus of a theoretical debate, clearly has a determining effect on much Italian poetry, during an era which sees a flourishing of innovative and experimental poetic writing.

Paragraph 33:2 (2010) 260–279
DOI: 10.3366/E026483341000088X

That crisis may be seen at work, often beneath the surface, in the poetry of the Orphic poet Dino Campana, whose concept of rhythm has not previously been the object of direct critical inquiry. Campana was certainly not alone in his struggles with rhythm, and with the difficulty of relating poetic rhythm to rhythm in the world. Eugenio Montale, for example, writing not long after Campana, famously laments his inability to capture his experience of the sea in successful rhythmical language, writing in the 'Mediterraneo' section of his *Ossi de seppia* (*Cuttlefish Bones*) (1925):

> Potessi almeno costringere
> in questo mio ritmo stento
> qualche poco del tuo vaneggiamento[1]

> (If only I could constrain
> in this my stuttering rhythm
> some small part of your raging)

Montale does not simply re-express the tired Romantic trope of awe in the face of nature, but rather suggests his disappointment that the natural world cannot be constrained by the limits placed on it by poetic rhythm.[2] Moreover, the sea fails to help the poet to understand how rhythm might work, other than to propose that the poet abandon traditional poetic constraints as the poem climaxes with the words 'Non ho limite' (I have no limits). This climax, however, is not a positive resolution but an expression of renunciation as the poet has lost all rational and emotional grasp on what he is able to do: 'Sensi non ho; né senso' (I have no senses; nor sense). This frustration at being unable to derive a poetic rhythm from an external phenomenon that one might have thought propitious to it is reinforced in the 'Motetti' section of Montale's later collection entitled *Le Occasioni* (*Occasions*) (1928–1939), in which he writes disparagingly of a dance rhythm, 'quest'orrida / e fedele cadenza di carioca' (this horrid / and faithful cadence of the carioca).[3] As Christine Ott outlines in her analysis of this poem: 'On the level of poetics, the "I" reflects (. . .) on how to translate adequately into words this rhythm of frenetic life'.[4] These examples from Montale's early poetic writings show the uneasy relationship between poetry, rhythm and the world during the early decades of the twentieth century in Italy. Montale is troubled by rhythm; but he is unable to shake it off. He continues to write both *in* rhythm (in the form of metrical, although free, verse) and *of* rhythm (as the examples above demonstrate). It seems impossible not to assume that both kinds of rhythm are essential to poetry — and that somehow, the external must be reflected in the internal. Yet how this might happen remains beyond determination. Similar difficulties may be found in the writing of D'Annunzio and of the Futurists, all of whom, like Campana, influenced Montale; and a wider study of the subject would certainly be rewarding. It is because his case is so exemplary that this essay will concentrate on the poetry of Campana.

Campana (1885–1932) published his only collection of poetry, the *Canti Orfici* (*Orphic Songs*), in 1914 following an intense period of wide reading (including Baudelaire, D'Annunzio, Nietzsche, Rimbaud and Whitman) and moving in Futurist circles in Florence.[5] His poetry vacillates between metrical verse, free verse and prose poetry. He talks explicitly of a 'ritmo sacro' (sacred rhythm), which remains as unattainable as a beautiful woman, as forbidden as the love of Dante's Francesca, and which reaches out to the poet even though it remains sacrosanct. He writes in 'La Verna — Ritorno':

sulle rive dei fiumi bevuti dalla terra avida là dove si perde il grido di Francesca: dalla mia fanciullezza una voce liturgica risuonava in preghiera lenta e commossa: e tu da quel ritmo sacro a me commosso sorgevi (*CO*, 45)

(on the banks of the rivers being drunk by the avid ground over where Francesca's cry disappears: from my childhood a liturgical voice rang out with a slow and moving prayer: and from that rhythm sacred to me, moved, you rose up)

Taking their cue from Campana, critics talk of 'the magical element which scans the rhythm of the orphic voyage' and of 'mysterious cosmic rhythms'.[6] These tantalising descriptions of rhythm do not, however, clarify what rhythm might mean for poetry. Rather, they show how the difficulty of using and understanding rhythm can translate into little more than a nebulous metaphor, in the absence of the question: where, and what, exactly, is the rhythm we are talking about? They also fail to explain the duality of Campana's rhythm. In Campana's work, rhythm is by no means always magic, mysterious, or cosmic. It can also be the opposite: earth-bound and spiritless, a 'ritmo affaticato' (tired rhythm).

Campana writes of how, as the world sleeps in silence, not knowing what the future holds, it nonetheless knows that rhythm will get going again as day breaks and noise returns. He writes in 'Genova':

> Dorme, dorme che culla la tristezza
> Inconscia de le cose che saranno
> E il vasto porto oscilla dentro un ritmo
> Affaticato (*CO*, 92)

> (It sleeps, it sleeps so that it lulls the sadness
> Unconscious of the things that will be
> And the vast port oscillates in a rhythm
> Tired)

Campana, according to Flavia Stara, 'focuses on this tired and melancholic rhythm, as if to use this absence of vibrations like a metronome through which he can continue to compose his symphony of travel'.[7] Once again the critic's analysis is problematic. Certainly, she is right to point out that the rhythm, here, is tired, and not magical, but she does not ask why. And once again, the critical metaphors used seem to have only a loose connection to the poetry itself: if rhythm is there, although tired, can we really speak of an absence of vibrations? Conversely, if rhythm is tired, can it really keep going at a regular, metronomic pulse to help the poet compose? Most importantly: is such regularity really what Dino Campana needs to compose his poetry? We will see that the opposite may be the case.

What this initial, cursory reading of Campana's poetry (and of the work of two Campana scholars) demonstrates is that rhythm is an unavoidable element of poetic writing, which may (but does not always) confer something sacred and mystical on language, but which risks tiring poetry out with an incessant beat. This twofold nature of rhythm — as both sacred and tired — is what orchestrates much of not only Campana's writing but also early twentieth-century Italian poetry in general. The hallowed rhythms of traditional verse remain an essential reference point, a necessary source of magic; and yet early twentieth-century Italian poets are all too well aware that such rhythms can also exhaust poetry.[8] The poet cannot sacrifice the mystery of poetic rhythm; but nor can he ignore the threat that it may have become worn out through over-use, a plod rather than an incantation. New strategies are needed to save it from itself.

Campana's work is unusually experimental with poetic form at such an early stage of the twentieth century in Italy; but it is also characterised by a dense network of images that clearly relate to the issue of how rhythm in the text might relate to rhythm in the world. I shall focus on two key features of his writing and how they affect ways in which poetry can be shaped by rhythm: verbs of motion, or the language of movement (especially the link between walking and writing), and fluidity of form (especially the metaphor of water). I will suggest that by exploiting metaphorical language that sets up a direct link with his experience of rhythm, notably metaphors of movement and fluidity, Campana puts rhythm into practice in his writing through syntax which is, itself, mobile and fluid. By developing a 'words in motion' technique, Campana finds a new place for rhythm in poetic language; one that was to influence later poets such as Montale who perceived, and exploited, the same two key features of Campana's writings that I shall explore.

In his essay on Campana in 1942, Montale writes of Campana's goal for poetry: 'the walk that Campana the poet in verse intended knowingly to carry out (...) had as its goal a complete colouristic-musical dissolution of poetic discourse'.[9] How might walking contribute to poetry's dissolving? This seems counter-intuitive; might not a regular walking rhythm have supported poetic metre? We will see why the contrary may be the case. Montale also describes this fluid language as 'colouristic-musical', possibly drawing on Campana's own description of his poetry as 'a European musical colourful poetry'.[10] Music, like walking, and perhaps painting too, is an activity that may be said to have rhythm, but a rhythm external to that of poetry. Is the specific rhythm of poetry itself in danger of being drowned out by those from outside?

Movement

In the course of Campana's relatively brief published collection of prose and verse poems, the *Canti Orfici*, the noun 'ritmo' (rhythm) only appears twice. These are the examples already cited: 'ritmo sacro' (sacred rhythm) and 'ritmo affaticato' (tired rhythm), from 'La Verna' and 'Genova' respectively. The adjective 'ritmico' (rhythmical) is also used twice in the penultimate poem of the collection, 'Piazza Sarzano' to talk of 'ritmiche cadenze mediterranee' (rhythmical Mediterranean cadences), which might remind us of Montale's rhythmic struggles with the sea; and 'un ritmico strido' (a rhythmical cry) (*CO*, 86–7). In two other poems which were not included in the *Canti Orfici*, 'Une femme qui passe' and 'Dall'alto giù per la china ripida', we find a further four instances of the word 'ritmo'. 'Une femme qui passe' (*CO*, 103) is an early poem, published posthumously by scholars who discovered it in Campana's notebooks. With its French title, the poem is a pastiche of Baudelaire's famous sonnet 'A une passante'. Campana writes here of a 'ritmo del passo' (the rhythm of walking-pace), a woman's walk which is 'solenne ritmico assorto' (solemn, rhythmic, lost in thought). The rhythm of her walk in fact poetically 'scans' (scandeva) her thoughts. As she walks, the woman leaves behind a mystery. Her walking creates a rhythmical patterning which is not simply that of the everyday; it transports instead into a mysterious realm:

> Une femme qui passe
>
> Andava. La vita s'apriva
> Agli occhi profondi e sereni?
> Andava lasciando un mistero
> Di sogni avverati ch'è folle sognare per noi
> Solenne ed assorto il ritmo del passo
> Scandeva il suo sogno
> Solenne ritmico assorto
> Passò. Di tra il chiasso
> Di carri balzanti e tonanti serena è sparita
> Il cuore or la segue per una via infinita
> Per dove da canto a l'amore fiorisce l'idea.
> Ma pallido cerchia la vita un lontano orizzonte.
>
> (A woman who passes by
>
> She went. Did life open up
> Before those profound and serene eyes?
> She went leaving behind a mystery
> Of dreams made real of which it is mad to dream for us
> Solemn and lost in thought the rhythm of her walk
> Scanned her dream
> Solemn rhythmic lost in thought
> She passed by. From amidst the noise
> Of jolting and thundering carriages serenely she disappeared
> The heart now follows her along an infinite path
> To where out of song and love the idea flourishes.
> Yet life is encircled by a distant pale horizon.)

Two important features of Campana's poetry are shown in this poem. The first is the use of verbs of motion (in this instance 'andare' (to go)); the second is repetition with variation (notably the transposition of the words of line 5 into those of line 7). These two features are not, in fact, separable. Campana uses verbs of motion because his is a poetry in motion, quite literally, in the way that he moves words around the page, repeating words in a new syntactical context. In fact, Eugenio Montale famously described Campana's poetry as 'una poesia in fuga, la sua, che si disfà sempre sul punto di concludere' (a poetry in flight, his poetry, which always undoes itself just at the point of concluding).[11] In the same way, solemn rhythm, rhythm as predictable regularity, whilst it sets the poetic dream in motion, later starts to unravel — before, perhaps, it tires itself and us.

The first three lines are written in a trisyllabic pulse which puts solemn metrical accents on the second of each group of three syllables (emphasis mine). The trisyllable had entered the Italian metrical canon via Palazzeschi; Campana mathematically squares this metre by making his lines nine syllables long:[12]

> Andava. La vita s'apriva
> Agli occhi profondi e sereni?
> Andava lasciando un mistero

Yet this regular pulse is undone as reality seeks to enter in the next line ('avverati'), disrupting the balanced metre. Regularity tries again to assert itself by maintaining the second-syllable emphasis of the trisyllable, but the pattern does not hold convincingly since the syllabic count is not a multiple of three ('Di sogni avverati ch'è folle sognare per noi'). After this uncertainty, rhythm is reconfigured; its relationship to metrical scansion is thematically reinforced (through the verb 'scandeva') but it becomes allied to a dream, as the adjectives 'solenne' and 'assorto', previously used to qualify the noun 'ritmo' are now recycled, together with the adjective 'ritmico', to describe the dream. The regular rhythm of the walk is clearly not unrelated to regular rhythm in poetry; but to become poetic as a subject, that walk must become lost in a thought that dissolves its rhythm; and the rhythm of the poem follows the same pattern. By sending rhythm on its way both metrically and thematically, that is to say, by not allowing rhythm to assert itself too forcefully as *either* metrical (the trisyllable) *or* thematic (the metaphor of walking), Campana signals that rhythm must disappear from the foreground, just as the woman herself disappears ('è sparita', itself is reinforced by the verbs of motion from the trisyllabic section, 'andava'). This is necessary if the mystery of rhythm is to hold. Movement, then, is a crucial element of the mystery of rhythm — and it is a movement which transports rhythm away from the domineering presence of emphatic stresses, and into a more subtle realm.

The same process may be observed in another early poem, 'Dall'alto giù per la china ripida' (*CO*, 110). It is in fact a preliminary version of a poem that was later revised and published in *L'Italiano* in 1929 with a dedication to the Futurist Marinetti under the title 'Traguardo' (The finish line) (*CO*, 111). In 'Dall'alto giù. . .', Campana writes of a 'ritmo infaticabile' (indefatigable rhythm), this time not of a woman, but of a cyclist ('corridore') in what seems to be a mountain stage of the 'Giro d'Italia';[13] though only later versions explicitly state that we are watching a bicycle race (another version of the poem was entitled 'Giro d'Italia in bicicletta' (Tour of Italy by bicycle)). The 'corridore' flies along ('tu voli') in a vertiginous descent ('Dall'alto giù per la china ripida'; 'Discende'; 'Vertiginoso'):

> Dall'alto giù per la china ripida
> O corridore tu voli in ritmo
> Infaticabile. Bronzeo il tuo corpo dal turbine
> Tu vieni nocchiero del cuore insaziato.
> Sotto la rupe alpestre tra grida di turbe rideste
> Alla vita primeva, gagliarda d'ebbrezze.
> Bronzeo il tuo corpo dal turbine
> Discende con lancio leggero
> Vertiginoso silenzio. Rocciosa catastrofe ardente d'intorno
> E fosti serpente anelante col ritmo concorde del palpito indomo
> Fuggisti nell'onda di grido fremente, col cuore dei mille con te.
> Come di fiera in caccia di dietro ti vola una turba.

> (From on high down the steep slope
> O cyclist you fly with indefatigable
> Rhythm. Bronzed your body from the whirlwind
> You come captain of the insatiable heart.
> Beneath the alpine rocks amidst the roar of the crowd starts up
>   [again
> For the life which was in the lead, the drunken dance.
> Bronzed your body from the whirlwind
> Descends throwing itself lightly
> Vertiginous silence. A rocky catastrophe burning nearby
> And if you were a serpent wheezing with the concordant
>   [rhythm of the untameable beating
> You would escape in the wave of the trembling roar, with the
>   [hearts of thousands with you.
> Like on a hunt behind you flies a crowd.)

The rhythm here is one that cannot stop, one that flies so fast that it barely knows what is happening to it. All it can do is to attune itself to the 'untameable beating' of the masses. As the rhythm races away at breakneck speed, it loses control of itself, and is no longer responsible for itself. This is perhaps why, after the first two traditional hendecasyllabic lines, the rest of the poem uncontrollably spills out beyond regular verse metre with the adjective 'Infaticabile' signalling the dissolution of rhythmical control.

Perhaps, on the thematic level, comparing this poem with 'Une femme qui passe', one could contrast the movement of walking, scanned by repeated beats, with that of a fluid downhill motion, as of a cyclist, requiring no such scansion, no such regular rhythmic segmentation. Perhaps this explains why, when he revised the poem, and made it explicit that what is going downhill is indeed a cyclist, Campana removed the word 'ritmo', and replaced it instead by the notion of movement, as is evidenced by the first four lines of the revised poem:

> Traguardo
>
> Dall'alta ripida china
> Movente precipite turbine
> Vivente nocchiero
> Come grido del turbine.
>
> (The finish line
>
> From the high steep slopes
> Moving precipitates whirlwind
> Living captain
> Like the shout of the whirlwind.)

Rhythm has been dissolved simultaneously in the greater fluidity of the new verse metre, and in the unscanned movement of the whirlwind or the cyclist; yet as with 'Une femme qui passe', as not a disappearance of rhythm, but rather its displacement to a less tangible realm, loosening its association with regular beats in the world outside.

Nowhere else in Campana's poetry do we find the word 'rhythm'. But his writings remain suffused with verbs of motion and diction of movement. We constantly encounter verbs such as 'andare' (to go), 'salire' (to climb), 'fuggire' (to escape), 'lasciare' (to leave), and we have seen some examples of these in the short extracts already cited.[14] These movements do not subdivide into the regular beats of footfalls. Nonetheless, they do continually evoke another kind of regularity which can be interpreted as analogous to scansion in poetry.

Departure and return, coming and going, are key themes in Campana's poetry of motion. The prevalence of these themes is made explicit not only by the titles of some of his poems, but also especially in the 'Ritorno' (Return) section of 'La Verna' (*CO*, 42–6), a prose poem inspired by the local Tuscan landscape in which Campana grew up.[15] As has already been seen in 'Dall'alto giù. . .', Campana closely associates writing poetry with his natural environment. The rocks that had surrounded the racing cyclist in that poem are present once again:

Ecco le rocce, strati su strati, monumenti di tenacia solitaria che consolano il cuore degli uomini. E dolce mi è sembrato il mio destino fuggitivo al fascino dei lontani miraggi di ventura che ancora arridono dai monti azzurri: e a udire il sussurrare dell'acqua sotto le nude rocce, fresca ancora delle profondità della terra. Così conosco una musica dolce nel mio ricordo senza ricordarmene neppure una nota: so che si chiama la partenza o il ritorno: conosco un quadro perduto tra lo splendore dell'arte fiorentina colla sua parola di dolce nostalgia: è il figlio prodigo all'ombra degli alberi della casa paterna. Letteratura? Non so. Il mio ricordo, l'acqua è così. (*CO*, 44)

(Here are the rocks, strata upon strata, monuments of tenacious solitude which console the hearts of men. And my fugitive destiny seemed sweet to me heading towards the fascination of the far-off mirages of adventure which still stream down from the blue hills: and to hear the whispering of the water beneath the bare rocks, still fresh from the depths of the earth. In this way I recognise a sweet music in my memory without being able to remember a single note of it: I know it is called departure or return: I know a painting lost amongst the splendour of Florentine art with its words of sweet nostalgia: it is the prodigal son beneath the shade of the trees of his father's house. Literature? I don't know. In my memory, that is what water is like.)

Movement in the natural world seems to give Campana impetus. The sound of water running down through the mountainous rocks calls him to his 'destino fuggitivo' (fugitive destiny). As Maura del Serra has observed in her analysis of 'Passeggiata in tram in America e ritorno', in the poet's 'destiny of flight' there is a 'necessary rhythm' which arises from his encounter with the movement of water.[16] This is articulated through a relationship between three verbs of movement: 'raccogliere' (to haul in), 'cullare' (to rock), 'rigettare' (to throw back out) (*CO*, 77). Water, like the cyclist, will flow downhill; but what goes down must come up. Similarly, in 'La Verna', movement, escape, departure, all come full circle, as departure is equated with return: 'so che si chiama la partenza o il ritorno' (I know that it is called departure or return). The subject of the verb 'si chiama' is supposedly 'una musica dolce' (a sweet music). Yet this sweet music — the sound of the water — is transposed into the interchangeability of departing and returning. The adjective 'dolce' of the 'musica dolce' (sweet music) is paralleled with the sweetness of his fugitive destiny ('E dolce mi è sembrato il mio destino fuggitivo') and the sweetness of nostalgia ('dolce nostalgia') which arises from the image of a painting of the prodigal son. Brought together by their sweetness, escape, music and nostalgia are vital analogies for Campana's poetic rhythm. All are connected with a coming and going; all are predicated on an endless cycle of departure and return.[17] Campana articulates the thematics of rhythm here not as an immediate analogue to metre, but as a cyclical patterning on a higher level. Whilst Campana may not be sure whether or not this kind of rhythm creates literature or poetry ('Letteratura? Non so'), it is clearly, nonetheless, the essential element of writing. Are we entitled to call it rhythm, since he does not, explicitly? We can at least see that it is a pattern into which what was previously called rhythm is sublimated.

Fluidity

As Campana writes two paragraphs earlier in 'La Verna — Ritorno':

Per rendere il paesaggio (...) ci vuole l'acqua, l'elemento stesso, la melodia docile dell'acqua che si stende tra le forre all'ampia rovina del suo letto, che dolce come l'antica voce dei venti incalza verso le valli in curve regali: poi che essa è qui veramente la regina del paesaggio.

(To render the landscape (...) you need water, the element itself, the docile melody of the water which spreads out among the channels into the wide ruins of its bed, which, sweet like the old voice of the winds, presses on down the valleys in regal curves: so that the water itself is indeed the queen of the landscape.)

Whilst he starts off by saying that you need water itself, this is in fact quickly transposed into its 'melody' (a melody nonetheless without notes), which, in turn, is transposed into a fugitive movement (it presses down, or 'incalza'). Since (the music of) water for Campana is 'la partenza e il ritorno' (departure and return), then actually what he needs to depict water is 'departure and return'. Symptomatic of this 'departure and return' are his obsessive iterations, such as the repeated insistence on the word 'dolce' and the word 'acqua' (which is then substituted by words such as 'fuga', 'musica/melodia' and 'nostalgia/ricordo').

Campana's obsession with water is also rendered in the penultimate prose poem of the *Canti Orfici*, 'Piazza Sarzano' (*CO*, 86–7). Here he portrays a Genoan cityscape with a tower in which a bell ('una campana') is hidden, thereby subtly encoding his own name in the scene. Immediately following on from his name, he moves his angle of focus to a covered fountain which:

getta acqua acqua ed acqua senza fretta, nella vetta con il busto di un savio imperatore: acqua acqua acqua getta senza fretta

(spurts out water water and more water without haste, and at its apex the bust of a wise emperor: water water water it spurts out without haste)

This syntactical construction is typical of Campana — it is the same technique of repetition with variation that we have already seen in 'Une femme qui passe', for example. Here we have a piling up of the key word, 'aqua', which, by virtue of its identical initial and final vowel, elides itself into a fluid circular verbal movement. Placing extracts from two other poems alongside one another, we find the same carefully tempered Campanian syntax deployed where there is a watery metaphor:

> Sorgenti sorgenti abbiam da ascoltare,
> Sorgenti, sorgenti che sanno
> Sorgenti che sanno che spiriti stanno
> Che spiriti stanno a ascoltare... (*CO*, 28)

> (Springs springs we have to listen to,
> Springs, springs which know
> Springs which know that spirits are standing there
> The spirits are standing and listening...)

> O poesia poesia poesia
> Sorgi, sorgi, sorgi (*CO*, 103)

> (O poetry poetry poetry
> Spring forth, spring forth, spring forth)

The first excerpt, from 'Il Canto della tenebra', is a typical example of the Campanian 'words in motion' technique. The second excerpt is from an untitled early poem; whilst it shows a somewhat stuttering naivety, this nonetheless serves to reinforce the relationship that Campana perceives between the liquid element and poetic language. Whereas in 'La Verna — Ritorno', Campana had revealed his uncertainty about the relationship between the writing of water and the status of his writing as literature, here in 'O poesia' the close alignment of a verb of motion specifically driven by water ('sorgi') alongside 'poesia' clearly grants a certain status to water in poetry.

Water becomes the allegorical medium par excellence for the patternings of movement which give life to poetic writing. But even in scenes where no water is to be seen, we find the natural ebb and flow, the departure and return, the circularity which characterises its rhythm. For example, Campana writes in 'Pampa' (*CO*, 71–3):

I miei pensieri fluttuavano: si susseguivano i miei ricordi: che deliziosamente sembravano sommergersi per riapparire a tratti lucidamente trasumanati in distanza, come per un'eco profonda e misteriosa, dentro l'infinita maestà della natura.

(My thoughts fluctuated: my memories followed on from one another: which deliciously seemed to submerge themselves in order to reappear in places rendered lucidly superhuman and far-off, like a profound and mysterious echo, from within nature's infinite majesty.)

Campana describes here an experience derived from his time travelling in the Pampas in 1907, recalling what he had perceived when lying down at night in pampas grass looking up at the starry sky. 'L'eterno errante' (the eternal vagabond) hears nature calling out to him — a call which is in fact a recall ('un richiamo'). This recall is present in the text itself by the obsessive repetitions of certain phrases, patterned also by the 'ora (. . .) ora (. . .) ora' (now (. . .) now (. . .) now), and enabled by the reluctance to close the sentence (punctuated instead with colons or an ellipsis):

Che cosa fuggiva sulla mia testa? Fuggivano le nuvole e le stelle, fuggivano: mentre che dalla Pampa nera scossa che sfuggiva a tratti nella selvaggia nera corsa del vento ora più forte ora più fievole ora come un lontano fragore ferreo: a tratti alla malinconia più profonda dell'errante un richiamo: . . . dalle criniere dell'erbe scosse come alla malinconia più profonda dell'eterno errante per la Pampa riscossa come un richiamo che fuggiva lugubre.

(What was escaping above my head? Escaping were the clouds and the stars, they were escaping: whilst in the trembling black Pampas which were running away at certain moments in the wild black race of the wind now stronger now weaker now like a far-off iron screeching: now and then a (re)calling to the most profound melancholy of the vagabond: . . . from the mane of the trembling grasses to the most profound melancholy of the eternal vagabond through the Pampas trembling again like a (re)call which escaped lugubriously.)

These prose poems, even more obstinately than Campana's verse, with their echoes of consecrated metrical patterns, refuse to tell us explicitly where exactly a sacred rhythm might be found, in the words or in the world they describe. Nonetheless, if we apply carefully the transformational technique suggested by 'Une femme qui passe' and by the metamorphoses of 'Dall'alto giù per la china ripida', we may suppose that we should see rhythm on two planes: as small-scale repetition, which is an essential building block of the poem, but would quickly become tired if left to dominate; and as a coming and going which absorbs the building blocks in a fluid operation, as of music, memory, or the natural movements of water. And this supposition, this transformation and absorption, is confirmed in 'Piazza Sarzano' where Campana describes hearing 'le ritmiche cadenze mediterranee' (rhythmical Mediterranean cadences). He is able to hear them because the physical make-up of the piazza creates an acoustical space in which a running child can be heard:

Sulla piazza acciottolata rimbalza un ritmico strido: un fanciullo a sbalzi che fugge melodiosamente

(In the resonant stony piazza rebounds a rhythmical cry: a boy darts across fleeing melodiously)

The cry rebounds; it echoes; and that, like footsteps (the boy, after all, is running), creates the kind of small-scale rhythm that Campana will label as such. It is, however, immediately recuperated into something larger and less structured: his flight becomes a melody. The echo does not remain merely an echo; it is transposed into a larger coming and going. That, we may say, is how its rhythm escapes becoming tired, and becomes sacred — sacred as music; and that process is mirrored in the patterns of the poem itself. Voices that sing, in Campana, are part of a greater melody that we cannot hear in its entirety; they are also patterned through a fluid, mobile syntax of repetition. In 'Il Viaggio e il Ritorno' (*CO*, 16), that pattern, that repetition with variation, is set off by the verb 'salire' (to rise up):

Salivano voci e voci e canti di fanciulli e di lussuria per ritorti vichi dentro dell'ombra ardente, al colle al colle.

(Rising up were voices and voices and songs of children and of lust through the twisted alleyways inside the burning shadow, towards the hill towards the hill.)

It is no coincidence that Campana uses a verb of motion to set off the movement of the syntax which is to ensue; and one which, like 'sorgi', implies an upward movement, as a counterpart to a downward one. Further syntactical variations continue throughout the rest of the paragraph, and each iteration is both a departure from, and a return to, the original formulation. This can be seen, for example, in the alliterative 'cantavano canzoni di cuori a catene' (they sang songs of hearts in chains), where Campana departs from the original noun 'canti' (songs / singing) and returns to it with a variation 'canzoni' (songs / love songs). This Campanian trait helps us to understand how rhythm works in the context of a poetry which is in the process of releasing itself from the shackles of traditional verse metre. Rhythm is in flight, a departure away from the original; but there is also, always, a return.

Setting out on his poetic journey, Campana is aware that the hallowed idea of a rhythm as a repeated cycle continually risks wearing the poet out. The greatest threat of exhaustion from within poetry would be the incessant accents of strict metrical form where no variation is permitted. In his octosyllabic verse poem 'La Petite promenade du poète' (*CO*, 31), the fatigue of metre becomes once again visible both in the poem's thematics, and in the apparent struggle of metre against its own rules. One has the impression that Campanian variation is trying to spark itself off from the repetition, but it cannot quite succeed: we end up with a dodecasyllabic line whose four-syllable anadiplosis, on the words 'via dal tanfo' (away from the stench), does nothing to assuage the incessant beat:

> Pur mi sento nella bocca
> La saliva disgustosa. Via dal tanfo
> Via dal tanfo e per le strade
> E cammina e via cammina
>
> (I even feel in my mouth
> Disgusting saliva. Away from the stench
> Away from the stench and through the streets
> And he walks and walks some more)

As in 'Une femme qui passe', walking seems to be a movement unable, on its own terms, to lend poetry to the scene. Indeed, the walking poet becomes so worn down by the beat which he cannot shake off that he ends up seeking relief by lying down like a dog at the side of the road ('mi ci stendo / A conciarmi come un cane'). The absorption into a higher pattern of departure and return had been disrupted by too incessant a beat.

When the walking poet sets off again in another verse poem, 'Batte botte' (*CO*, 54–5), this time he is less obviously bound by a strict metre. The verse line lengths move from four syllables to eight to five to three, although the four-syllable line remains the dominant one. The lines whose strict syllabic count is not four syllables could, however, be counted as four since the flow of enjambement allows for certain elisions.[18] Thus, for example, 'Splende un occhio / Incandescente' (Shines out an eye / Incandescent), if read with the elision permitted via the syntactical enjambement, would elide the first syllable of 'incandescente' with the last syllable of 'occhio', creating a regular rhythmical flow of four syllables per line (rather than a five-syllable line with 'incandescente'):

Splen | de un | oc | chio / In | can | de | scen | te
1   2   3   4 / 1   2   3   4

This more fluid interpretation of a 'strict' rhythm fits in with the presence of fluid vocabulary, set up in the very opening lines of the poem: 'Ne la nave / Che si scuote' (In the boat / Which rocks). This is then also reinforced by a direct reference to the water some lines later and through the positioning of the words 'passo' (step) and 'notte' (night) which are used in different syntactical positions throughout the poem (although always at a verse-line end, for the purposes of rhyme). The poet's path may be determined by the rhythm of his walking pace; but that rhythm echoes, like the rhythmic cry of the boy in 'Piazza Sarzano', within a larger space that subsumes it: here, the sea; and the sea not merely as the element to which all returns, but also as a source:

L'acqua (il mare
Che n'esala?)
A le rotte
Ne la notte
Batte (. . .)
Per le rotte
De la notte
Il mio passo
Batte botte.

(The water (the sea
What emanates from it?)
Along its routes
In the night

Strikes (. . .)
Through the routes
Of the night
My footsteps
Clip clop.)

The word 'rotte' implies not only the idea of a determined route, but specifically also of shipping lanes; thus the route of pre-determined footsteps which clatter along the road in a potentially dreary rhythm are re-configured as the fluid motion of a ship.

Similarly, the repetitive elements of music itself, in Campana's poetry, can be absorbed by the fluid. Musical rhythm depends, of course, on distinct notes; that is how it is always analysed and notated. But Campana's poetry, just as it turns footsteps into melodies, elides the distinctiveness of notes. Like the woman in 'Immagini del viaggio e della montagna' (*CO*, 47–9) who 'A le melodie della terra / Ascolta quieto' (To the melodies of the earth / Listens in silence), the poet also listens so that 'le note / Giungon, continue ambigue come in un velo di seta' (the notes / Arrive, continuous ambiguous like in a silk veil). Immediately following on from this attentive listening to the melody of the natural world, poetry emerges in a fluid torrent: 'Da le selve oscure il torrente / Sorte' (From dark woods the stream / Emerges). The veiled reference to the opening lines of Dante's *Inferno* confirms that this fluid poetry, for Campana, emerges from nature: 'Nel mezzo del cammin di nostra vita / mi ritrovai per una selva oscura' (Midway through the journey of our life / I found myself in a dark wood).[19] Following the path of the revered poet, Campana allows his own poetry to flow out. This acknowledgement of the revered fluidity of poetry (and the significance of the reference to Dante) is reinforced in 'La Verna — Ritorno' when he writes 'Dante la sua poesia di movimento, mi torna tutta in memoria. O pellegrino, o pellegrini che pensosi andate!' (Dante his poetry of movement, all comes back to me. O pilgrim, o pilgrims who go pensively!)

The explicit references to rhythm, in Campana's poetry, tend to be to a kind of rhythm that is destined to be transformed or absorbed in poetry, and never to dominate it alone: the repetitive rhythm of the footfall or of the immediate echo. That is analogous to strict, repeated, poetic metre, which, left to its own devices, would tire out poetry itself, as well as the poet and his reader. But there is a higher kind of rhythm. It is analogous to the first in the fact of its beat, its coming and going; but its movement is not tangibly regular. It happens in a less calculable time. It echoes, not human activity, but the fluid movement of water; or melody, music conceived not, precisely, as articulated rhythm, but more as continuous development; or the operation of memory. Where words are in motion, where poetry is fluid and dissolves the regular without forgetting its obligation to return, that is where 'sacred' rhythm resides.

Campana's use of the word 'ritmo' and its cognates raises an essential question for the possibility of writing about rhythm. I have distinguished between two types of rhythm: the tired, and the sacred. The former is an unproblematic category in that it corresponds to traditional definitions, and is also labelled rhythmic by Campana himself. But the latter he often seems to avoid calling by that name. He does so at least once, in the expression 'ritmo sacro', and he creates a unique and admirable ambiguity around the word in 'Une femme qui passe'; but at least once, too, as we have seen, he erases the word 'ritmo', it would seem to avoid giving it the sacred, fluid sense. Are we entitled, then, to call that fluid coming and going, which remains essential to poetry, 'rhythm'? I think we have to; we have no other word for it, and its relation to the first kind of rhythm is such that it deserves to be recognised in a common name. We will allow ourselves, then, to say that there is a second kind of rhythm, a higher rhythm, which cannot easily be perceived in the present moment of writing (or reading) poetry. It goes via another, longer path. Even as Campana shifts between verse and prose poetry, he acknowledges that this higher rhythm — notwithstanding its distance or intangibility — remains an absolutely essential element of poetry; it is as essential to our existence as water. Rhythm in poetry must not make its presence too insistent, as theme or as prosody, because otherwise it risks becoming worn out (like the incessant beat of the 'Petite promenade du poète'). But carefully veiled within metaphors of movement and fluidity, music and memory, it opens up spaces for the articulation of something sacred that is the very essence of poetry.

NOTES

1 Eugenio Montale, *Tutte le poesie* (Milan: Mondadori, 1990), 60. All translations my own.
2 According to Christine Ott, 'the voice of the sea represents an ideal which already by then could only be cited in a nostalgic retrospective' (Christine Ott, *Montale e la poesia riflessa: Dal disincanto linguistico degli 'Ossi' attraverso le incarnazioni poetiche della 'Bufera' alla lirica decostruttiva dei 'Diari'* (Milan: Franco Angeli, 2003), 115).

3 Montale, *Tutte le poesie*, 143. Ott explains that the 'carioca' was 'a very popular dance at the time' (*Montale e la poesia riflessa*, 156).

4 Ott, *Montale e la poesia riflessa*, 157.

5 Campana had entrusted his manuscript to Florentine Futurist Ardengo Soffici in the hope that Soffici might publish it. Soffici lost Campana's original (and only) manuscript, which was entitled *Il più lungo giorno*, a phrase borrowed from a 1910 novel by Gabriele D'Annunzio, *Forse che sì, forse che no*. Campana had to re-write his collection of poetry from memory, publishing it at his own expense under the new title *Canti Orfici*. In the 1970s the original 'lost' manuscript was found and critics were able to establish that the *Canti Orfici* are not only a tour-de-force of memory (although a number of sections are significantly different) but also contain a number of new poems. The edition referred to throughout is *Canti Orfici e altre poesie*, edited by Neuro Bonifazi, which also includes Campana's unpublished poems in the 'altre poesie' section (Milan: Garzanti, 1989). Whilst published translations of the *Canti Orfici* do exist (such as Charles Wright's *Orphic Songs* (Ohio: Oberlin College, 1984)), many of these do not also include the unpublished poems. All translations, therefore, are my own. This edition of *Canti Orfici* will be abbreviated to *CO* throughout.

6 Flavia Stara, *L'Incanto orfico: Saggio su Dino Campana* (Bari: Palomar, 1997), 66; Cesare Galimberti, *Dino Campana* (Milan: Mursia, 1967), 91.

7 Stara, *L'Incanto orfico*, 152.

8 Italian poetry, like French poetry, is syllabic. The traditional, 'hallowed' verse metre is the hendecasyllable.

9 Eugenio Montale, 'Sulla poesia de Campana', originally published in *L'Italia che scrive* (1942), reproduced in *Montale Il Secondo Mestiere: Prose 1929–1970*, edited by Giorgio Zampa, 2 vols (Milan: Mondadori, 1996), I, 577.

10 See Carlo Pariani, *Vita non romanzata di Dino Campana* (originally Firenze: Vallechi, 1938, then Milano: Guanda, 1978).

11 Montale, 'Sulla poesia de Campana', 574.

12 Montale describes this rhythm as 'passando vicino all'esperienza ritmica palazzeschiana' (passing close to the Palazzeschian rhythmical experience), since Palazzeschi is renowned for his trisyllable lines ('Sulla poesia de Campana', I, 577).

13 The 'Giro d'Italia' was inspired by the 'Tour de France', and the first Giro took place in 1909.

14 These are in fact the four most frequently used verbs in the *Canti Orfici*. A frequency analysis of the volume reveals that 'andare' (in its various conjugations) is the most commonly-used verb throughout.

15 See also, for example, 'Il Viaggio e il Ritorno' (The Journey and the Return Journey) (*CO*, 16–18) and 'Passeggiata in tram in America e ritorno' (Tram Journey in America and Return Journey), *CO*, 77–78.

16 Maura del Serra, *Dino Campana* (Florence: La Nuova Italia, 1985), 85.
17 As Giuseppe Ungaretti writes in the final couplet of his 1916 poem 'Nostalgia': 'E come portati via / Si rimane' (And as if transported elsewhere / One stays behind), cited in *Poesia italiana del Novecento*, edited by Edoardo Sanguineti, 2 vols (Torino: Einaudi, 1969–71), I, 854.
18 As Alberto Bertoni states: 'in the *Canti Orfici*, there is a very high frequency of enjambement, almost 20% of the collection; (...) enjambement which is so systematically and deliberately used within a free-verse mechanism indicates that free verse belongs to the domain of poetry — of poetry and the necessity for the poet not to renounce the creation of effects of anticipation or lack of resolution of the rhythmic nodes within verse or macrostructural elements', in 'Appunto sul metro degli "Orfici"' in *Dino Campana alla fine del secolo*, edited by Anna Rosa Gentilini (Bologna: Mulino, 1999), 121–33 (131).
19 Dante, *Inferno*, Canto I, lines 1–2.

Unfree Verse: John Wilkinson's *The Speaking Twins*

SIMON JARVIS

Abstract:
This essay revisits the relationship between philosophy and poetry. It argues
that a crucial term, 'verse', is often missing from discussion of that relationship.
The broader term, 'poetry', is so difficult to define that it offers insufficient
specific resistance to large philosophical schemas. The question is explored here
through an analysis of the prosodic microstructures in John Wilkinson's *The
Speaking Twins*. I conclude that Wilkinson's poem is an instance of 'unfree verse'
(in a sense which I define in the essay) and that the poem's verse technique is
also the site of its historical truth-content.

Keywords: versification, free verse, philosophical poetics, rhythm, metre,
Adorno, 1980s

What follows is an essay in philosophical poetics. But it wants to speak,
not about the relationship between philosophy and poetry, but about
the relationship between philosophy and *verse*.[1]

This might sound like a category-mistake. 'Verse', for many ears,
perhaps, names just that part of poems which has the smallest connection with thinking, with knowing, and therefore with philosophy.

Why might this term be needed, then? 'In Shakespeare's poems',
says Coleridge, 'the creative power and the intellectual energy wrestle
as in a war embrace. Each in its excess of strength seems to threaten
the extinction of the other.'[2] It is not the division between creation
and intellect that I want to endorse, but the idea of the 'war embrace'
itself. 'Each in its excess of strength seems to threaten the extinction
of the other.'

This is where we come to the trouble with 'poetry'. It is very hard
to know what it is. So whatever it is would already be a philosophical
question. What poetry is would be something to be determined by
philosophy. In practice this has meant that it can generally be defined
by imagination, by metaphoricity, by defamiliarization, or by whatever
the philosopher likes. Meanwhile, whatever philosophy is would not
be a poetical question. What philosophy is would not be something

Paragraph 33:2 (2010) 280–295
DOI: 10.3366/E0264833410000891

to be determined by poetry. The term, poetry, is already too weak for the war embrace. It has little specific resistance — it has difficulty squeezing back.

Verse, meanwhile, resembles, in its relation to philosophy, an almost infinitely unimportant and yet inconveniently specific object. It is some grit that has got into the machine. It is a matter of interest to note how many of the major philosophical authorships feel obliged at some point to say something about it, in a way which must feel merely peculiar to modern philosophers, for whom philosophy rarely has a more necessary relation to verse than it would have to pirouettes or to patisserie. It is a matter of further interest to note how often this grit, even when the philosopher is doing nothing more than clearing it out of the way, tells us something important about their whole project.[3]

Let us take one example — not merely any example, but perhaps one of the most significant engagements with poetry on the part of a philosopher to have appeared in the last century. In Martin Heidegger's essay 'Language', he develops the counter-intuitive ideas that 'Language speaks', and that, indeed, it speaks us. He develops this thought by meditating on a poem by Georg Trakl, 'Ein Winterabend'. He quotes the poem, and an alternative version of its last six lines, and then comments thus: 'The poem is made up of three stanzas. Their meter and rhyme pattern can be defined accurately according to the schemes of metrics and poetics.'[4] Although this can be done, there is no good reason for Heidegger to do it, because:

The content of the poem might be dissected even more distinctly, its form outlined even more precisely, but in such operations we would still remain confined by the notion of language that has prevailed for thousands of years. According to this idea language is the expression, produced by men, of their feelings and the world view that guides them. Can the spell this idea has cast over language be broken?[5]

But before we follow Heidegger in his attempt to answer this question, we should note what has already been decided. Metrics and poetics are species of knowing. As such, they may be correct, but do not matter. As knowing, they must, as always in Heidegger, stand lower than thinking. The concepts of metrics and poetics are, then, not really territory for thinking. They raise no philosophical questions; they are simply classifications.

What has happened here? In the same philosopher's essay on 'The Origin of the Work of Art' we have one of the most powerful and consistent attempts extant to dismantle the presupposition that works of art, and indeed, for Heidegger, that *poems*, eminently, have nothing to do with knowledge. Towards the end of that essay we can hear, even, of the importance of a thingliness of poems, of their tones and perhaps even their tunes, as well as of their words and their thoughts. Yet here, and in every other place where Heidegger refers the paralinguistic and extralinguistic elements of verse to knowing and not to thinking, a kind of Platonism wins out within the very heart of the process which is supposed to be repeating and dismantling it. The poems are handed over, again and again, to paraphrase. Their thinking, however, is happening not only, or even primarily, in what can be paraphrased. It is happening also, or even primarily, in that thingliness which Heidegger's own thinking about works of art seemed perhaps more likely than any other among his contemporaries to unseal.[6]

I should want (with many others, perhaps) to contend that it is just this resistant remnant, what cannot be paraphrased, which, to use Heidegger's own language, calls for thinking. In order to attempt such thinking, I am going to try some self-criticism.

In 1990 I wrote a short review of a poem by the British poet John Wilkinson. My own first experience of his verse was at a public reading which he gave. I vividly recollect the way in which an initial bafflement, indeed anger, which I experienced at the levels of semantic, narrative and thematic dislocation that I was being asked to process gave way to what felt not like what we are so often told we are supposed to feel in the presence of non-paraphrasable verse, a disturbance or a subversion or an emancipation from various of our presuppositions—to feel, indeed, just what we are supposed to feel in the presence of fundamental *philosophical* questioning — but, instead, something like an underlying momentum, a momentum working above all at the level of the intersection of the individual speaking voice with a series of rhythmic and syntactical recurrences and differences. The stuff of it seemed in a singular way at once too rhythmically aberrant to produce anything like a metrical set, and *also* too insistently recurrent, too preoccupied with the fine collisions of repetition and difference to languish into inert arrhythmia. But when I tried to write about Wilkinson's astonishing longish poem of that year, 'The Speaking Twins', none of this could make it into my account. Instead I took a thematic and lexical route, through the poem's preoccupation with twinning and with oppositions, and with 'stars' whether astronomical, typographical (asterisks) or of stage and screen.[7]

Certainly it is essential to sketch the semantic and thematic penumbra which surrounds or hovers inside the poem. Much of it is an unmarked dialogue in which two unnamed polemicists mutually tease and harangue each other. Their voices virtuosically resist social, geographical or sexual placement, transiting effortlessly from blunt materialism to refined conceptuality or, no less effortlessly, yoking the two together: 'Freedom eats odours into its carpet', notes one of them. The voices circle towards a less exhausted sense for some concepts which might seem all ready for philosophy to grab: notably, of 'freedom' and 'humanity'. Yet as soon as philosophy does try to grab them they turn back into the ineffably tedious items they were before, when philosophy already had possession of them.

This, then, is the point at which it becomes essential to try to lay hands on the technique itself. The lines race forward in threes. They remind us of a kind of blank terza rima, because despite being stripped of what Mandelstam described as Dante's 'arsenal' of interlocking rhymes, they nevertheless gather a kindred momentum.[8] There is no absolute syllabic or accentual constraint, yet there appears to be no simple absence of or freedom from these constraints either: most of the lines look roughly the same length on the page and the majority of them cluster in the range between nine and thirteen syllables; the majority of them offer us between four and six accentual peaks.

It is in this context that the idea of 'unfree' verse surfaces. It quickly becomes clear that there is nothing corresponding to what could be called a 'metrical set': that is to say, there is no system of recurrences which becomes rapidly enough established for a skilled performer to relate it to some metrical design or other in which he or she might already know how to perform.[9] For example, whereas a 'metrical set' would allow some disambiguation of metrically ambiguous monosyllables such as 'all' or 'is'—and how often, in fact, the tension between rhythm and metre in metrical verse is repeatedly evoked and brought to bear centrally on the semantic content at precisely such monosyllables—there are in this poem even fewer guides to intonational melody than ordinarily exist in a writing system which accords to intonation little more than the highly approximate sketches given by punctuation markings, or, as it used aptly to be called, by 'pointing'. This, of course, is also often the case in metrical verse, because decisions about metrically ambiguous polysyllables are very often not disambiguated by metrical set, and so they become closely bound up with questions of rhetorical organization (one thinks of the word 'so' in Milton) or of thematic interpretation ('all' in Shakespeare's sonnets). Here in this poem, even the weak assistance offered by metrical set to intonational disambiguation is absent.[10]

How, then, does one account for the powerful experience of momentum produced by this poem? One initially obvious route — to determine the numbers of stresses in each line in order to see whether, if there is not anything so clear as a metrical set, there might nevertheless be other forms of recurrence and patterning — in fact faces difficulties. As Viktor Zhirmunsky observed in his important article on 'The versification of Majakovski', the absence of a clear metrical set itself means that 'statistical counts of the number of stresses will be subject to very substantial variations'.[11] In metrical verse a kind of metrical autodisambiguation is generally at work. But absent a metrical set, the interpretation of metrically ambiguous syllables becomes still more clearly an art rather than a science — and, in the limit cases, can become a matter of readerly discretion, so that not only can radically divergent 'delivery designs' (Fowler, following Jakobson) be adopted for the same poem, but many more options are open in individual delivery instances.[12] The question of the patterns of stresses present, already a problematic one even in relation to metrical verse, is therefore made almost intolerably difficult to answer because of the absence of the intonational disambiguation which a metrical set can offer. Nevertheless, what can be heard even from a first silent performance to oneself (and then confirmed by comparative analysis with passages of Wilkinson's prose) is that the ratio of relative stress peaks to syllables is much higher than that in prose, and comparable to that in the leading heritage art-verse metre, the heroic line.[13] Wide as the range of possible performances is in heroic-line poems, the range is much wider here, because the absence of metrical set creates a completely different relation between word-stress and phrasal stress than that which operates in metrical verse.

Here is the beginning of the main body of the poem proper, after a short introductory section:

★ ★ ★ ★ ★ ★ ★ ★ ★ ★ ★ ★ ★ ★ ★

Stars come over coy against the ghostly light we
blotted them out with, into the yellow–dark
integument of latex, wrinkled flat by sodium

dabbing stars like sperm droplets till their hiss
of insignificance pinned back, refaced us all
down with a black lustre, sheening to trans-

lucence under no star sailing out that curves
taut over the scrubbed snarls of shadow-fax,
roughing bone up. Around us, the Cherenkov light

If the three-line groupings and the poem's opening recall Shelley's 'Triumph of Life', this passage prepares the elements of a latter-day 'Julian and Maddalo'. That earlier poem can move with no sense of strain from dialogue to landscape description and back again. Here, we are being readied for an argument between two voices, intensely virtuosic, compressed and complex, yet also uncontextualized and uncharacterized: the writing is not organized so as to allow us to conjecture the sex or class, much less the psychological singularity, of these 'speaking twins'. For the Venetian sunset of Shelley's poem, we have, here, a setting which is a kind of suppressed cosmos. The sky is 'yellow-dark' from sodium lighting, and so the stars can hardly be seen. The poem interprets this not as an undesirable yet unintended consequence of the need for proper street lighting, but rather as the very end aimed at by street lighting. The stars are 'pinned back', 'blotted out.' The sky is an 'integument of latex', as though this sodium lighting were pushing a rubber sheet flat against the sky in order to conceal it. This perhaps suggests the next figure for the stars: they are 'like sperm droplets'. The sodium lighting is a kind of contraceptive, designed to prevent these stars from procreating. The setting, in fact, is the strenuously achieved cocoon of would-be pure culture, in which the work of screening out the cosmos, with its unbearable reminder that we do not make culture in circumstances of our own choosing, is never done. In this dome of worked light, we are not so much lit as 'refaced (. . .) down with a black lustre'. The stars are still there, and we know it, yet we have done our best to push them to the very edge of the world, a state of denial captured by the contradiction of negation and verb here: 'under no star sailing out that curves'. If there is no star, how can it sail out? Yet no other subject wields the verb. Chérenkov light is 'visible radiation produced when charged particles traverse a medium which increases their initial velocity to a velocity greater than that of light' (*OED*, 'Cerenkov'); it is emitted from nuclear-power reactors, but can also be used to determine the properties of cosmic rays and supernova remnants. We are indeed, in this yellow-dark night, walking under the negation of a star: in a world in which we may determine the properties of stars with unprecedented precision, yet rarely catch a glimpse of them ourselves. And the line of asterisks with which the introduction is marked off from the main body of the poem gives us a shrunken print of the stars.

When we come to consider the metrico-rhythmic properties of this passage, one thing which is immediately evident is the infrequency of punctuation and its non-coincidence with line-end. Derek Attridge, in his Warton Lecture for 1988, suggested that verse lies on an axis between 'internal segmentation', in which the division of language into lines or other segments is perceptible even without a text, and 'external segmentation' in which it is nearly or entirely impossible to determine where language is segmented without a written or printed cue. As he emphasizes, this distinction is not the same as that between metrical and non-metrical verse, even though it is sometimes taken to be so. Whitman's largely non-metrical verse, for example, is strongly internally segmented, because of the marked degree of coincidence between line breaks and syntactical and/or rhetorical ones. Many passages of *Samson Agonistes*, on the other hand, despite its metricality, are hard to segment simply from a heard performance, because in a metrical poem of variable line length there is a number of possible options for segmentation.[14] Indeed, this can be the case even in a metrical poem of fixed line length, such as Shelley's *The Triumph of Life* — an important presence behind *The Speaking Twins* — in which, in one passage, a strong counterpoint is set up between the ten- and eleven-syllable heroic lines which are the poem's principal metrical set, and a series of six-syllable groups of a rising rhythm which, in this passage, are strongly marked out by rhetorical and syntactical parallelism cutting against the written layout:

> But I, whom thoughts which must remain untold
>
> Had kept as wakeful as the stars that gem
> The cone of night, now they were laid asleep,
> Stretched my faint limbs beneath the hoary stem
>
> Which an old chestnut flung athwart the steep
> Of a green Apennine: before me fled
> The night; behind me rose the day; the Deep
>
> Was at my feet, & Heaven above my head[15]

The last four phrases set up a clear rhythmic counterpoint, thus:

> Before me fled the night;
> Behind me rose the day;
> The Deep was at my feet,
> & Heaven above my head

Here, therefore, two 'metrical sets' are, briefly, operating simultaneously. What this reminds us of is the instability of the idea of metre itself. Metre is always suspended between induction and deduction, description and prescription, because it is always something which you have both to induce empirically from the verse material in front of you (otherwise you could just decide that it was in any metre you liked) and also something which you have to *do* to the verse material in front of you (a metrical performance does not result simply from obeying the ordinary phonological rules for the organization of intonational patterns in everyday speech, but is, on the contrary, always an attempt performatively to reconcile two often conflicting sets of requirements: the requirement of intelligibly organized phonology and the requirement that the line count as an instance satisfying a set of underlying rhythmic constraints). There is a necessary circle here: you cannot make the poem work metrically without making a decision about its metre, but you cannot make a decision about its metre without already having made it work metrically.

On this axis, Wilkinson's poem is clearly a long way towards the 'externally-segmented' pole. Yet these external segmentations also leave their mark on intonation, and therefore on metrico-rhythmic texture. This can best be appreciated by considering the melodic differences made by segmentation to syllables which might ordinarily be unstressed or which might ordinarily be metrically ambiguous. At the end of the first line, the word 'we' falls into the category of what Marina Tarlinskaia's exhaustive work on the metrical values of monosyllables in English verse calls 'words which accentually vary within the level of (. . .) both strong and weak stress', that is to say the most metrically ambiguous category of all.[16] If we were to retranscribe the first two lines of Wilkinson's passage as prose, 'Stars come over coy against the ghostly light we blotted them out with, into the yellow-dark', most deliveries would not stress the personal pronoun. Yet as printed, the case is not so clear. The existence of a number of lines of roughly the same printed length and within a limited range of numbers of strong stresses induces some sense in the reader that the line is really a line, that it does not only have graphic but also metrico-rhythmic significance. For this reason it is, experience suggests, hard to read these two lines in just the same way as one reads them when printed as prose. Yet if one offers a marked stress in order to mark line-end, this too creates difficulties because of the unwanted and irrelevant rhetorical implications: a marked stress on a personal pronoun implies, as Tarlinskaia's classification indicates, that the pronoun is being used in opposition to some other pronoun: *we* blotted the stars out, but *you* just left them alone. The case of 'all', at the end of the fifth line of the passage, is similar: it is difficult to swallow 'all' up as we would were this not verse, and yet to foreground it with a strong stress seems to say 'it refaced us *all* down, you know, not just some of us'.

These kinds of moment of course are very frequent in non- or parametrical verse in which violent enjambement (here: between subject and verb ('we/blotted'); between adjective and noun ('yellow-dark/integument') often recurs. Yet they have the more force here because of the suspicion of a shadow of metre which I mentioned earlier. Other elements gradually come to reinforce this suspicion: strong stresses begin nine of these seven lines, and are strongly prevalent in this place in much of the poem. Meanwhile, many of the lines also close with stresses, so that line breaks typically become something like sites of jammed stress, where one stress clashes up against another at the beginning of the next line. At the same time, the infrequency of pointing means that line-breaks sometimes take on that quasi-syntactical function which they often have in blank verse with a great deal of run-on (in much of Wordsworth's or Shelley's blank verse, for example): retranscription as prose reveals that many of the component clauses of these sentences would be almost breathless were they not in verse. 'Wrinkled flat by sodium dabbing stars like sperm droplets till their hiss of insignificance pinned back' is a mouthful. Yet it does not, as it happens, get to be less of a mouthful by being verse. No good reader is likely to take a big gulp of air at 'hiss', I suggest, because the damage to the clause's continuity would be too great: a breath here would be almost comical. The passage produces instead the simulacrum of a chance to breathe, and *foregrounds* in this way the poem's breathlessness. The poem shares that characteristic of Shelley's style whereby a syntactically and rhetorically and argumentatively generated momentum keeps running into and through recurrent traps for attention in the instrumentation (here, e.g. the 'hiss of insignificance pinned back' where we find a number of the devices enumerated by Brik[17] all at once: not only the obvious assonance of /i/ but also the asymmetrical chiasmus of 'h*i*ss' and 'ins*i*gnificance' (asymmetrical because stressed in the first case and not in the second), not to mention the consonance between the endings of the same two words. Wilkinson has dropped Shelley's rhyme and loosened his constraints on syllable-number, and yet the linguistic material feels, if anything, more cut into and cut up, more deliberatively *deformed* by verse, than Shelley's.

The poem is arranging, in fact, for line-endings to become moments of powerful intonational complexity and ambiguity. This is intensified when the segmentation of linguistic material which happens at the end of lines starts to cut up the words themselves. At one point the line is broken in the middle of a word, albeit at a morphologically motivated point: 'trans-/lucence.' Here too, prose intonation is interrupted so that 'trans-' attracts emphasis. This is a reasonably containable case, because the word is easily broken at this point and because one can imagine a certain thematic rationale for the break: by it, the poem adds one item to its heap of disappointing *Ersatz* light-substitutes: lustre, sheen, -lucence. Later, though, something much less familiar, and apparently quite mannered, happens:

> Say why you twisted your neck like a human
>
> squeaks? Coming hard on a backbone, feel the
> same infatuate, the same fell. Where the sec-
> retary of darkness, tugged her head at the f-
>
> irst edge that was sensible, was found in mother's
> necktie, plunging from her low, kindly neck.

The segmentation in the third and fourth lines of this passage cuts deeper than 'trans-/lucence'. 'Sec-/retary' dissects the 'secret' in 'secretary', while 'f-/irst' is the hardest of all these cases to rationalize, because it cuts into the syllable, the sacred cow of some metrical primers.[18] 'f-', the phonemic scrap, is part of its line, but would not show up in a syllable-count. Conversely, just as the line is violently cutting into linguistic material in this way, in a way which has the appearance of declaring and enacting the sovereignty of the line, despite its metrical variability, over word and syllable, the line itself is under attack, because majuscules keep being allowed to erupt in the middle of it:

> Confecting in polyps, curveting in charged nodes,
> discharged in a flashy advertising How *too much:*
>
> never had been heresies but Index first causes,
> cells passed in a dataStream to founTainhead None
> calls but hears on his own frequency, Enter

The effect appears to begin as a response to the prosodic energies of branding: the mid-word majuscule attention-grab in 'dataStream' is apparently mimicked and mocked in 'founTainhead', yet has also migrated into the articulation of Wilkinson's lines themselves: 'Enter', 'None', and 'Index' all appear with initial capitals, yet do not follow full stops. One way of thinking about this is to recall how often upper- and lower-case at the beginning of lines operated in the twentieth century as tribal badges, symbols or exponents held forth shewing the kind of thing the reader could expect to get (loosely and yet by no means reliably, metrical or non-metrical); Wilkinson retains the initial lower case, but, because he permits upper-case for reasons that are not perfectly syntactical, a mutilated figure for the possible co-evality of rhythmic organization with linguistic material is pinned into the poem.

While these features of Wilkinson's mode of segmentation, then, might no doubt in one kind of interpretation feature as an ultimate refusal of a phonocentrism putatively lingering even in non-metrical verse, I think that would be too quick. In the passage about the necktie there is clearly the possibility of following through or working up a series of mimetic connections, because of the thematic attention to suicide by asphyxiation. But if breathlessness is concentrated there, it would not because of any putatively naturalistic illustration, but because this passage brings to a climax (a 'squeak') a collision between momentum and the need to pause or draw breath which has been working powerfully since the poem's opening lines.

It is, in fact, almost as though the writing were setting out to refuse two competing ideas of metrico-rhythmic expressiveness, ideas which had mostly managed to operate an excluded middle through twentieth-century Anglophone poetry — an idea, in the first place, according to which rhythmic expressiveness is absolutely dependent upon the prior existence of metrical constraints which alone make rhythmic micro-structures even perceptible, let alone expressive or significant; and another, opposite idea, according to which metre is and can only be a system of *restrictive* constraints which must rule out sectors of the spectrum of rhythmic expressiveness which could otherwise be allowed to become available. Few poets, and perhaps, few living individuals as such, have ever believed exclusively in either of these options; rather, the questions of metre and rhythm in contemporary poetics and poetry feel permanently unsolved yet immovably blocked, rather as the fundamental questions of metaphysics have sometimes been left blocked yet unsolved by the claims of professional philosophers that these questions are 'poorly formed' and should therefore be deleted from the roster.[19]

And perhaps this is where the notion of 'unfree verse' can come into focus. The poem is written at the end of what was perhaps a uniquely damaging decade for certain kinds of humane and liberal values, the

1980s, a decade in which the word 'freedom', made to rhyme with private property over and over again, shrank to that near-perfect depthlessness it has ever since retained. Of course the connection between political and verse freedom, between free verse and freedom proper, has only ever been a fantasy, yet, because it is the case that all verse effects have to be fantasized before they can become real, because all verse works not by a quasi-medical operation upon the etherized reader but by inducing in readers some matching performances of virtuosic fantasy,[20] the connection sticks around: and it is as though, in this poem, the sinews or wiring of verse were to register both the flatness of being free in verse only, and the deadness of a compensatory and resentful remetrification. Might Wilkinson's 'unfree' verse in fact register, not at the level of attitude or opinion — *the poet's opinions*, that perfectly insignificant item — but, instead, with the suffering-desiring-thinking body of its immersion in technique, a series of experiences at once too elusive and too painful to be thematized? Out of this immersion emerge fundamental words, mutilated and transfigured and suddenly worth thinking about again. 'Say why you twisted your neck like a human/squeaks':

Humanity'

s the alternate self-same, never so complete
Opposite which opposites packet to grip

in a cannibalized topographical sheet of latex.

The scission of humanity just at its elision with being, the copula, produces a kind of para-intonational squeak or gulp where an apostrophe is invited, impossibly, to end the line, as though 'the human' were to reside not in that ancient heirloom, the rationality of the rational animal, but in this paralinguistic gasp. It is as if in the poem's so-called technique were registered both the nullity of current soundings of the words freedom and humanity, and the falsehood of the despair which would therefore delete them. One recalls Jacques Roubaud's description of Denis Roche's project as a 'critique of free verse... which is not a destruction of free verse, but a destruction of what is not free in free verse'.[21] This apparently technical innovation, completing the work on technique taking place through the poem, might, then, be the site also of its most penetrating thinking. In this isolated apostrophe is heard both the falsehood of a secure humanism of the rational animal and the twinned falsehood of its anti-metaphysical and anti-humanist antagonists.

I should like to conclude with two wider points. First, on verse and language. If we are to hear the thinking in verse we have decisively to reject one prevalent false diagram of its relationship to language. According to this diagram, verse is a subset of literary language, which is itself a subset of language in general. This diagram assumes that we know what language is, where it starts and where it stops, and so that it is meaningful to describe verse as a subset of a subset of this set. Whether or not we all know exactly what language is, where it starts and where it stops, verse is not in any event a wholly contained subset of it. Language is one of the materials of verse. Others are paralinguistic or extralinguistic — rhythms which do not merely derive from language, but which are imposed on it in a series of transformative mutilations. What results, as Allen Grossman once forcefully pointed out to me, is no longer, only, language. This is why Zhirmunsky's insistence, contra Jakobson, that verse makes a *selection* from language, rather than doing 'violence' to it — gives us only half the truth. The fact that language cut up is no longer only language produces the whole interest of the interpretation of verse by philosophy, an interpretation which has always to operate across a deep unlikeness of kind.

This brings me to my second suggestion. If there is to be a real relationship between philosophy and poetry, it must be one in which poetry can sometimes think better than philosophy, or at least think things that philosophy cannot. This is one problem with philosophical aesthetics as the means of managing that relationship: in it, philosophy is the knower and art is the known. Only where philosophy can find out from poetry something which it could not in any case have made earlier for itself, something which poetry thinks and has been enabled to think through its technique, can we witness Coleridge's antagonistic and resuscitating 'war embrace'.

NOTES

1   The conception of philosophical poetics from which I start develops from a reading of T.W. Adorno's *Aesthetic Theory* and its place in the German philosophical tradition. I attempt to set out some of its main features in 'The Truth in Verse? Adorno, Wordsworth, Prosody' in *Adorno and Literature*, edited by David Cunningham and Nigel Mapp (London and New York: Continuum, 2006), 84–98.

2   S.T. Coleridge, *Biographia Literaria*, edited by Nigel Leask (London: Dent, 1997), 191. I elaborate further on the significance of this remark for the

relationship between philosophy and verse in the 'Introduction: poetic thinking' to *Wordsworth's Philosophic Song* (Cambridge: Cambridge University Press, 2007), 1–32.

3   For some examples, see Immanuel Kant, *Kritik der Urteilskraft*, section 43, where 'prosody and metre' figure as a kind of reliquary for the free spirit of art, which would otherwise evaporate into mere play; Hegel's extended treatment of versification in his lectures on fine art (which I discuss in 'Musical thinking: Hegel and the phenomenology of prosody' in *Paragraph* 28 : 2, special issue on 'The idea of the literary', edited by Nicholas Harrison (July 2005), 57–71); Schopenhauer's account of metre and rhyme as 'fetter' and 'veil' in chapter 37 of *Die Welt als Wille und Vorstellung*. (For a rebuttal of Schopenhauer by a poet-critic, see David Samoilov, *Kniga o russkoi rifme* (Moscow: Khudozhestvennaya Literatura, 1973), 4; I was led to Samoilov's work by Barry P. Scherr, *Russian Poetry: Meter, Rhythm, and Rhyme* (Berkeley and London: University of California Press, 1986).) In each case the question of verse as technique opens up substantive and central problems in the broader ontologies of art and beyond art offered by each thinker, as I attempt to show for Hegel in 'Musical thinking'.

4   Martin Heidegger, 'Language', in Heidegger, *Poetry, Language, Thought*, translated by Albert Hofstadter (New York: Harper and Row, 1971), 189–210 (195).

5   Heidegger, 196.

6   Martin Heidegger, 'Der Ursprung des Kunstwerkes', in *Holzwege* (Frankfurt am Main: Vittorio Klostermann, 1994), 1–74. For an earlier argument about Heidegger's failure to pay attention to poetic technique as a mode of cognition, cf. T.W. Adorno, 'Parataxis. Zur späten Lyrik Hölderlins', in *Noten zu Literatur* (Frankfurt am Main: Suhrkamp, 1974), 447–91. The continuing consequences of such an oblivion or relegation of technique for the thought even of philosophers wishing to argue that art is a mode of knowledge are vividly evident in, for example, Alain Badiou, *Petit manuel d'inesthétique* (Paris: Seuil, 1998). The claim that 'It would not be difficult to say what art knows' is followed by an account of Mallarmé which depends almost entirely on paraphrase, so that the difficulty of saying what art knows *as art* is not solved but set aside.

7   The short notice was published in *Equofinality* 3 (1990). For important remarks introducing Wilkinson's 1986 sequence *Proud Flesh*, but with significance for his authorship as a whole, see Drew Milne, 'Introduction' to *Proud Flesh*, second edition (Great Wilbraham: Salt Publishing, 2005), ix–xvi. Milne argues against any recuperation of Wilkinson's poetry as 'lyric': it appears 'both to affirm and to undermine the centrality of lyric impulses' (xiii). The psychoanalytic commentator and essayist Adam Phillips, suggesting that *Proud Flesh* is a 'great contemporary text', speaks of Wilkinson

as 'writing a haunting, unheard of lyric poetry against the grain of the taught traditions' (rear cover); Wilkinson's own powerful literary criticism was collected recently under the title *The Lyric Touch* (Great Wilbraham: Salt Publishing, 2007). The present essay deliberately leaves untouched the question of the pertinence of the concept of 'lyric' to Wilkinson's verse. For useful commentary on metrico-rhythmic aspects of some recent British poetry, see Lacy Rumsey, 'Formal innovation in non-mainstream British poetry since 1985', *Etudes anglaises* 60 (2007), 330–45, and 'Form before genre: "free verse" and contemporary British poetry', *Etudes britanniques contemporaines* 26 (2004), 73–91.

8   Mandelstam, 'Conversation about Dante', in *The Complete Critical Prose and Letters*, edited by Jane Gary Harris, translated by Jane Gary Harris and Constance Link (Ann Arbor, Michigan: Ardis, 1979), 397–442 (397).

9   For 'metrical set', see Roger Fowler, 'What is metrical analysis?' in *The Languages of Literature: some linguistic contributions to criticism* (London: Routledge and Kegan Paul, 1971), 141–77.

10   Compare Clive Scott's remarks on the greater importance which 'paralinguistic' elements take on in the scansion of French *vers libre* when compared with French metrical verse: the scansion of free verse 'needs to become a method of describing disagreement, ambiguity, textual metamorphosis; it needs to come to grips with the recitational and paralinguistic, precisely because free verse dispenses with the neutral corner, wishes itself an unmediated utterance; it needs, for these purposes, to create new scansional concepts and a terminology to go with them' (Clive Scott, *Vers libre: The Emergence of Free Verse in France 1886–1914* (Oxford: Clarendon Press, 1990), 24).

11   Victor Zhirmunsky, 'The Versification of Majakovski', in *Poetics. Poetyka. Poetika*, 2 vols (Warsaw: Państwowe Wydawnictwo Naukowe and The Hague: Mouton, 1961–6), II, 211–42 (227). For useful applications of a statistical method to some non- or para-metrical verse in English, see G. Burns Cooper, *Mysterious Music: Rhythm and Free Verse* (Stanford, California: Stanford University Press, 1998).

12   Roger Fowler, 'What is metrical analysis?', 142–3. See also G. Artobolevskii, 'Kak chitat' Mayakovskoyu' in *Mayakovskii 1930–1940. Stat'i i materiali*, 278–9; quoted by Zhirmunsky, 230.

13   I prefer this eighteenth-century term to the phrase 'iambic pentameter' because the latter seems to me a misleading term for the metrical set usually labelled thus. The question is still open and cannot be laid to rest here (for a sceptical account, see Peter L. Groves, *Strange Music: The Metre of the English Heroic Line* (Victoria, BC: University of Victoria, 1998); for a foot-scanning approach, see George T. Wright, *Shakespeare's Metrical Art* (Berkeley and LA: University of California Press, 1988). Derek Attridge prefers the term

'five-beat rhythm' (*The Rhythms of English Poetry* (London: Longman, 1982), 123–44).

14 Derek Attridge, 'Poetry Unbound? Observations on Free Verse', Warton Lecture on English Poetry, read 13 January 1988, *Proceedings of the British Academy* 73 (1987), 353–73.

15 Text from Donald Reiman, *Shelley's 'The Triumph of Life': A Critical Study* (New York: Octagon Books, 1979), 137–8.

16 Marina Tarlinskaia, *English Verse: Theory and History* (The Hague, Paris: Mouton, 1976), 76 ff.

17 Osip Brik, 'Zvukovye Povtory' (Sound Repetitions) in *Two Essays on Poetic Language* (Ann Arbor: University of Michigan, 1964), 1–45.

18 The technique can also be found in some poems by John Weiners.

19 See the arguments against such deletions of metaphyiscal questions in T.W. Adorno, 'Meditationen über Metaphysik' in *Negative Dialektik* (Frankfurt am Main: Suhrkamp, 1973), 354–400.

20 This is an argument which I have recently developed in work on Alexander Pope's handling of rhyme and sound repetition, drawing on some remarks made by Roland Barthes in *Le plaisir du texte*.

21 Jacques Roubaud, *La Vieillesse d'Alexandre: essai sur quelques états récents du vers français* (Paris: Éditions Ramsay, 1988), 157 (my translation).

Notes on Contributors

Helen Abbott is Lecturer in French at Bangor University. She researches rhetoric, poetics, music and aesthetics in France and Italy 1850–1950, with particular emphasis on theories of voice. She is author of *Between Baudelaire and Mallarmé: Voice, Conversation and Music* (Ashgate, 2009).

Peter Dayan started academic life as a specialist in nineteenth-century French poetry. His recent research has concerned the reasons for which, from the Romantics to the 1960s, poems are described as music, paintings as songs, symphonies as poems, and so on. He is the author of *Music Writing Literature, from Sand via Debussy to Derrida* (Ashgate, 2006); he is currently writing *Art as music, music as poetry, poetry as art, from Whistler to Stravinsky* (to be published by Ashgate in 2011). He is Professor of Word and Music Studies at the University of Edinburgh.

David Evans is Lecturer in French at the University of St Andrews. He works on rhythm, form and musico-literary relations, especially in the nineteenth century, and has published *Rhythm, Illusion and the Poetic Idea: Baudelaire, Rimbaud, Mallarmé* (Rodopi, 2004) and articles on Michel Houellebecq, Théodore de Banville, Debussy and the French-language poetry of Corsica.

David Gascoigne is Honorary Senior Lecturer in French at the University of St Andrews. His research hitherto has centred on twentieth-century French narrative, including books on Michel Tournier and on Georges Perec and ludic fiction.

Simon Jarvis is Gorley Putt Professor of Poetry and Poetics in the Faculty of English at the University of Cambridge, and a Fellow of Robinson College. Among his publications are *Adorno: A Critical Introduction* (Routledge, 1998) and *Wordsworth's Philosophic Song* (CUP, 2007), as well as many essays on the poetics of verse.

Paragraph 33:2 (2010) 296–297
DOI: 10.3366/E0264833410000908

Carolina Orloff is a researcher in Latin American literature at the University of Edinburgh. She recently completed her PhD on Julio Cortázar and the representations of the political in his fiction. She has also published on translation theory and is currently working on twenty-first-century Argentinian literature and film.

Eric Prieto is an Associate Professor at the University of California, Santa Barbara, where he teaches French and Francophone studies. He is the author of *Listening In: Music, Mind, and the Modernist Narrative* (Nebraska, 2002), and is currently finishing a book project titled *L'entre-deux: Literature, Geography, and the Postmodern Poetics of Place.*

Barry Scherr is the Mandel Family Professor of Russian at Dartmouth College in Hanover, New Hampshire, USA. He has published articles on a wide range of topics dealing with Russian poetry and prose, with special interests in Russian verse theory, the works of Joseph Brodsky, and literary figures of the early twentieth century. His books include *Russian Poetry: Meter, Rhythm, and Rhyme* (University of California Press, 1986); *Maksim Gorky: Selected Letters*, co-edited and co-translated with Andrew Barratt (Clarendon Press, 1997); and, with Nicholas Luker, *The Shining World: Exploring Aleksandr Grin's 'Grinlandia'* (Astra Press, 2007). His most recent article, 'Chukovskij's Whitmans' (2009) traces how the selection, the ordering and even the texts of Kornej Chukovskij's translations evolved as he introduced Walt Whitman to Russian readers in editions published over seven decades.

Emma Sutton is Senior Lecturer in the School of English at the University of St Andrews, Scotland. Her principal research interest is musical-literary relations in the late nineteenth and early twentieth centuries. Her publications include *Aubrey Beardsley and British Wagnerism in the 1890s* (OUP, 2002) and essays on Mark Twain, Vernon Lee, Henry James and Victorian poetry. She is completing a book on Virginia Woolf and music and is editing *The Voyage Out* for the Cambridge University Press scholarly edition of Woolf's work.

EU Authorised Representative:

Easy Access System Europe Mustamäe tee 50, 10621 Tallinn, Estonia

gpsr.requests@easproject.com

Printed and bound by CPI Group (UK) Ltd, Croydon, CR0 4YY

09/06/2025

01897301-0001